Hooligan

Paddy Holohan was a mixed martial artist before the revelation of a life-threatening blood disorder forced him to retire in 2016. He is now the owner and manager of the mixed martial arts facility and community centre SBG D24 in west Dublin, and is a newly elected councillor for Sinn Féin.

Richard Barrett is the cofounder and COO of Pundit Arena.

Hooligan

Paddy Holohan

with Richard Barrett

Gill Books

Gill Books
Hume Avenue
Park West
Dublin 12
www.gillbooks.ie

Gill Books is an imprint of M.H. Gill and Co.

978 07171 8628 0

Design and print origination by O'K Graphic Design, Dublin
Printed by CPI Group (UK) Ltd, Croydon CRO 4YY

This book is typeset in 13.5/17 pt Minion.
Title and chapter headings in Frutiger Light.

The paper used in this book comes from the wood pulp of managed forests. For every
tree felled, at least one tree is planted, thereby renewing natural resources.

A CIP catalogue record for this book is available from the British Library.

5 4 3 2 1

PROLOGUE

I spat the blood and gravel out of my mouth. It tasted like cement on my tongue. Dazed, I looked down at a tooth lying on the floor. 'At least you got away,' I thought to myself.

My head throbbed, but I had come to know that feeling very well. 'You've got plenty left in ya, Paddy,' I told myself as I gathered up every ounce of energy in my thin body. I lifted myself up off the ground again and, blood oozing from the cuts on my face, I spat out the same words one more time.

'Is that all you've fucking got?'

I walked towards the source of my pain, and it happened again. Whack. And I dropped to the floor.

'Somebody take this ginger lad away, he's crazy.'

As I lay on the ground, I rubbed my tongue through my mouth, counting and nervously searching for another hole, but the rest of my teeth were still there. 'I barely felt that fucking one,' I laughed, staggering to my feet like an alcoholic who's reached rock bottom. But this wasn't my rock bottom.

This was the day Paddy fucking Holohan announced his arrival to the people of Jobstown.

Ten years old, I wouldn't allow myself to be bullied anymore.

It was time for the Hooligan to take over.

Round 1

CHAPTER 1 ....

T he battlefield of my youth was Dromcarra in Jobstown, in the south-west of Dublin, one of the most disadvantaged areas in Ireland. A government housing project gone wrong, a Darwinian jungle of a council estate where there was one rule: adapt or die. Natural selection was alive and well in Jobstown, and I was starting off at the bottom of the ladder.

Jobstown was cast aside on the outskirts of the M50 motorway, which had a twofold effect on the people who lived there. It taught us that we were different and, because we had been pushed out of the city, we all grew up with a chip on our shoulder. But it also helped to bring the community together. Yes, we fought each other day-to-day, but if an outsider threatened another Jobstownian, they'd have the whole estate after them. It's a very Irish attitude. We're incredibly self-deprecating, but if an outsider challenges or offends us, that's when we come together. Tallaght was like its own little country in Dublin, and Jobstown, for me, was its capital.

As much as I loved Jobstown, living there was tough and caused me constant anxiety growing up. This government project had failed and created a dystopian environment where success levels were low. People from Jobstown had a 10% chance of going to university. Just six miles down the road in Terenure, that number was six times bigger. Jobstown was an anomaly in Dublin for all the wrong reasons. I guess you could say I grew up in hell, six miles from heaven.

No one would have believed that I'd become a fighter. I had a fiery attitude, but I couldn't really fight. In Jobstown, if kids were getting bullied at home, they'd come outside and take it out on someone else on the road. That's just the way it was. I often ended up as the target but it only made me stronger. When I was about ten years of age, I fought a guy on my road and he just kept dropping me, but I continued to get up and move forward. He'd drop me again, and I'd get up again. And again and again and again. It got ridiculous to the point where he just wouldn't hit me any more. I kept going at him, and he eventually had to ask people to bring me home. I wouldn't stop, I was going to kill him. That was me, a gladiator stuck in a jockey's body.

I learned pretty quickly that being a Holohan meant having a tough life. Life was full of inconsistencies, but trouble was the one constant. The same could be said for the life my mother lived; she was always battling uphill.

On 3 May 1988, a baby was born in the Coombe Hospital in inner-city Dublin to Vera Holohan, a single mother from a working-class background. Births like this were a regular occurrence in 1980s Ireland despite the oppressive efforts of the Catholic Church, but the arrival of Patrick Pearse Holohan was not. I was different right from the start. Had I been aware of the struggles that were to follow in years to come, I might have retreated back into my mother's womb at that very moment, but I was born a fighter, and fighting is what would come to define me.

My mother was one of six kids. Her father, my grandfather, was in the army and away a lot of the time when she was growing up, and my mother left school early to help her own mother at home. She fell pregnant when she was young and spent time in the Magdalene Laundries, and sadly, her baby did not survive. She also lost another baby a few years later when my brother Neville died. Neville is buried in Glasnevin baby's garden, but I didn't know anything about him for years and it really upset me when I found out. My mother is a strong woman, and the trauma didn't deter her from trying to have another child. Thankfully she gave birth to my sister Marguerite in 1980 and I was born eight years later. She would never get over the loss of her children, and those tragedies marked the beginning of her battles with mental health. That constant struggle has been a part of my mother's life for as long as I can remember, and it saddens me when I think of the tough times she's been through. She's never had an easy life, something that had an effect on my own upbringing and a childhood that was less than ordinary.

I don't know how she did it at times. My mother was raising two kids on her own and was on social welfare. She didn't really have an education and worked as a cleaner in a bike shop every so often – that's the only job I remember her having. I know she loved me and only wanted the best for me and for Marguerite, but I now realise that the environment we grew up in would be considered a neglected one. I didn't know any different at the time and I sometimes wonder how I got through it all. We grew up on welfare and that was it, St Vincent de Paul blankets and hampers at Christmas. It was nothing to be ashamed of. Jobstown was all about survival.

I grew up without a father, but I didn't notice it as much as you would think. I was angry and upset, but not to the point where

I thought about it every minute of every day. The shame of having a child out of wedlock was something that my mother could never shake. A generational thing, undoubtedly; I gave less of a fuck. I lived in an area where single-parent homes were commonplace. Lots of us didn't know our fathers, so why would I have a right to feel different?

There must have been something in the air in Dublin during the late 1980s because there was an explosion of births in the Jobstown area, which meant there were lots of kids around my age growing up. We were flat broke but at least we had each other. A lot of my friends were my guardians — my gang, if you must — and we always had strength in numbers.

From the time we were five or six, we were raised on the road. We were put out on the street. We knew every nook, every pothole. The street was part of us, our proving ground, whether that was through football or fighting, and the muck field in Jobstown, known as 'the Muckers', was our Colosseum.

Once, when I was around thirteen, I got into a fight with a guy. I ended up catching him and dropping him before putting him in a sharpshooter, a move I had only ever seen watching WWF wrestling on TV. It was crazy looking back. I was trying to submit this guy and knew absolutely nothing about submissions. But, as was the case in most housing estates, the older brother was never too far away. He ran up and kicked me as hard as he could, right in the face. I don't know whether I was knocked out, but I remember crawling to my friend's garden. As I tried to escape, I could see Sean, my good friend and neighbour, sprinting towards the brother like Linford Christie. He had seen what happened and went straight for him. Boom, boom. Sean lit him up. That's how it was in Jobstown, we stuck together.

That field held so many memories for us as kids. We drank. We dabbled in drugs. We learned what hash was, boys selling five spots, ten spots. The sharpshooter, though, that was talked about for days. Those days shaped me, in good and bad ways.

I wasn't able to evade every beating. Our road didn't get on with other roads, and the shop was the meeting point for them all. You couldn't be on your own at the shop, or else you were definitely getting into a knock or a bit of a hiding. One time a guy got off the bus in his work gear, Snickers pants and all, and immediately began running at me.

'You hit my little brother, ya prick.'

I protested my innocence but it was no good. He grabbed me by the ear and took a bite out of it, blood rolling down the side of my face, but my beating wasn't over yet. He dragged me to the front door of a house on the road, looking for a young fella the same age as me so that he could give me a hiding. There I was, deep in enemy territory, blood dripping down my back, waiting for a fella to come out to fight me. Luckily, the boy wasn't at home, so the other lunatic gave me a kick up the hole and sent me home.

The worst thing was that when I went home, it felt like no one noticed these things. I turned up covered in blood with a piece of my ear missing, but my mother barely batted an eyelid. She was too busy doing her own thing to process what had happened, away in her own world. Part of me didn't care, because I was always trying to hide things from my mother.

At that age, I was so frustrated. I would sit in my room and I'd smash a pillow, smash a wall, and tell myself, 'When I get older, this bullying is going to stop. I'm going to change the way people treat me.' I couldn't take my anger outside to the road, because I was so small. It would have just made the situation worse. I know how to fight now but it wasn't always like that. I had friends who would look after me, some of whom I'm still close with today. Two of them, Wayne and Sean, ended up robbing a bank and being sentenced to eight years in jail. Wayne is a good guy but he was a bit of a bully. He'd grab you and hit you, but Sean would stick up for me and tell him to leave me alone. Sean was a big lad and could knock a grown man out. I used to look up to him, and even today we're still close. But he had his own stuff going on as well, and you could get a hiding off him too. In Jobstown, you never knew.

I don't know if my mother's situation got worse as I got older, or I just became more aware of it, but she began to really struggle with raising two young kids. I was often left to fend for myself, with only Marguerite to look after me. Marguerite is a tough motherfucker, the strong one in the house. Growing up wasn't easy for her either. She took on a lot of the responsibilities in our house from a young age, a lot of the work that my mam should've done, and I was always grateful for it. Even though we had different fathers, I always felt close to her. I'm a living example of the old saying that it takes a village to raise a kid. The people of Tallaght raised me, I took little pieces from everyone, and there were a lot of people without whom I would not have made it. Marguerite was one of those.

Marguerite's love was tough love, and it was the only love I felt as a young child. She was the enforcer of the house; my first black eye was from her. She'd fight on the road, and broke her wrist one day fighting a fella. She had no problem knocking people out, even me. Running down the stairs, I called her a tramp, and she hopped an aerosol can off my head. I remember waking up at the end of the stairs, dazed and confused, but knowing never to call her that word again unless I was outside of throwing distance. That was life in my house. I was a little bollocks, and if I told my ma to 'fuck off', Marguerite would slap me in the face. My ma never told her to stop.

It was often like I was on my own in the house. My mam and Marguerite had their family before I came along. Marguerite had said things like that to me growing up — 'Everything was great before you came along' — and she was probably right. They lived in a flat in Avonbeg, another part of Tallaght, and had to move to a bigger house because of my arrival. Marguerite resented the fact that they had to move and the disruption that it caused, but to be fair, she was only a kid herself at the time.

It reached a point where things got so bad for my mother that Marguerite and I were sent into care after school. I hated it so much. We were looked after by a woman in a house up the road from ours, and I remember being there with two African lads, questioning why my mother didn't want us around. I treated the woman poorly, and one day, she took her frustration out on me and struck me in the face twice. I was six years old, in a strange place, and I still remember the impact of the clatter I got. It shocked me but I did everything I could to hold back my tears. Show no weakness, that was my way of thinking. Marguerite grabbed me, gave the woman a mouthful and we walked out of the house, never to return again.

My mother wasn't well mentally, and I've been dealing with that all my life, but she never hit me as a child. She didn't really drink, and was far from an alcoholic, or abusive, but she depended on state-commissioned antidepressants and painkillers prescribed by doctors that were too busy to see what her real problems were. She had dealt with so much trauma in her life and needed counselling, not a steady stream of prescription drugs. She was experiencing the stigma associated with raising two kids out of wedlock, losing two children, and growing up in an area rife with stress and frustration. As the doctors kept prescribing her pills, I watched each one chip away at her mind. She did her best for us, even if it wasn't enough. She's incredibly brave and strong, and I love her dearly.

When I was born, I was the man of my house and that was it. I grew into that role out of necessity and as soon as I could start doing things around the house, I did. I still did some mad things, though. I remember arranging to buy a horse in Smithfield with one of my friends, Stephen Dunne. I gave him half the money and he came back the next day, turned up at nine in the morning with a horse.

'Is Paddy there?'

We had a scratching pole and all in the back garden, apples and oats too. If my son brought a horse to the door as a ten-year-old, I'd lose it with him, but my ma barely questioned what was going on.

'Ah it's grand, Ma. He's only here for a few days.'

It's moments like that where I look back and wonder if it was negligence on her part, allowing me to do those things. I wasn't an angel, I was an angry kid, but some of the other kids on the estate were pure evil. Being constantly in that environment out on the street was hard, it gave me anxiety, but it wasn't impossible. Some guys really had it hard where they were going home to alcoholic and abusive parents. Some were dealing with sexual abuse in their own homes, but I didn't know it at the time. As the years passed, some of these kids that I knew ended up in mental institutions. Others are not around any more.

They didn't make it and I understand why. If my house had been as hard as the road and I had nowhere to go for a break, away from it all, I don't know if I would have made it either.

It's not the positives from my childhood that I remember most vividly. It's the sound of a man's knuckles smashing a woman's cheekbone into pieces or the cries of help that reverberated around the estate whenever my cousins felt the wrath of a dysfunctional, alcohol-fuelled marriage. My cousins were close to me in age, location, and friendship, but if I had a tough upbringing, theirs was significantly worse to the point that most of the kids didn't survive it, not in a way where they were able to get on with their lives. My aunt and her husband would drink to excess and often fall onto the street physically assaulting each other, but those were the good times because it meant they weren't beating my cousins. The eldest daughter of the family couldn't take the constant chaos and ran away to Northern Ireland to live with my other aunt, Margaret, when she was sixteen.

'Pack up your stuff, come live with me, and no one will take you back to that the house again.'

To this day, she never returned to her house. She ran away and never came back, and I don't blame her.

The tension heightened around special occasions. Christmas meant one thing; alcohol was in the house. We used to think it was great in a way because the parents would be out fighting in the middle of the night while my cousins and I, no more than ten years old, would crack open a can and share it between us. I remember one Christmas Day, my aunt's husband started attacking my aunt outside on the road. The whole estate could see it. He had my aunt by the hair, punching her in the face while my ma was on his back, trying to pull him off. She was always jumping in for her sister, and got clipped herself. I stood on the porch watching it unfold, frozen with fear, but even as a kid, it was always a case of 'if you're hitting one of my family members, I'm coming for you.' I picked up a stick and ran over to help my ma. I hit my uncle over the head, but it only made things worse and my cousin started fighting with me. He felt he had to; I'd hit his father.

The memory of the first time that I saw what life was really like in my cousins' 'home' still haunts me. We were just kids and I remember sneaking down to their house in the middle of the night to play with my cousins. We probably made too much noise but I could hear my aunt screaming up the stairs. I hid in the wardrobe, hoping not to be seen, but she came into the room and leathered those kids with a bit of bamboo that she had. In the wardrobe, petrified, I urinated myself. I sat there for over five minutes, drenched in a mix of urine and tears as she unloaded shot after shot on my cousins' bare skin. I still remember the sound of each shriek. I always will.

Moments of madness were a regular part of my childhood. I didn't know they weren't the normal actions of a parent. I didn't know how a dad was supposed to treat his kids; I never had one. Those days were tough on me but even tougher on my cousins. One of them took to heroin and never came back. His brother burned down the family home while he was still in it. Twice. His body survived, but his mind didn't, and he's still in a care home.

My cousins told me to forget what I had heard from the wardrobe that night.

'Don't say it to anyone on the road, please.'

And I didn't. I had no one to confide in, not my family, not my friends, and I just stuffed the memory deep into the back of my mind, repressing it along with every other fucked-up part of my upbringing. But I'm running out of space and something needs to give. I have to shine a light on the darker moments of my life because I'm not sure if I can keep them in any longer.

CHAPTER 2 ....

For the first nine years of my life, I didn't know that I had a potentially fatal blood condition. When I found out, nothing changed. I lived in one of the craziest places in Ireland, got cuts and bruises almost every day. I jumped off walls, got in fights and did all of the things a wild young kid would do. It was pretty reckless. I was a loose cannon and could've died at any minute, but sure what did I care? Death never scared me.

When I was seven years old, I was out on the back field with some of my friends throwing stones, one of our favourite things to do at that age. Out of nowhere, a stray brick came hurtling towards my head. Bang. Direct hit. I didn't think much of it at the time, other than the fact that it hurt like fuck, but I was definitely a bit dizzy. The dizziness got worse to the point where I felt like getting sick, so I went home to lie down on the couch. I could feel myself getting more and more tired. I didn't know it but the brick had caused a blood clot in my jaw. While I was lying on the sofa, it travelled up to my brain. I told my mother and my aunt Margaret that I wasn't feeling well.

'No, you're grand,' Aunt Margaret said, trying to keep things calm. 'He's just been throwing stones,' she reassured my ma.

My ma saved my life, though. She had heard that there were a few cases of meningitis around the estate and, worried, she phoned an ambulance straight away. I was rushed to Our Lady's Children's Hospital in Crumlin, where I passed out in the waiting room. From that point on, I can only remember two things: waking up after my surgery, and one other moment that will stay with me for the rest of my life.

There was no MRI scanner in Our Lady's Hospital at the time, so when I collapsed in the waiting room, they put me in a helicopter and rushed me to Beaumont Hospital on the other side of the city. The seriousness of my condition quickly became clear, and I needed emergency brain surgery to save my life. I was kept in an induced coma while the surgeon cut through the bone of my skull and took the blood clot from my brain. At first, it seemed the surgery had gone as well as it could have gone, but another blood clot on my brain burst and in the middle of the night, I was rushed back in for a second surgery. I feel I can remember the whole thing, that operating theatre, so vividly. I stood in the corner of the room, an out-of-body experience, looking at my tiny, lifeless body in my underpants on the bed with tinfoil wrapped around me and the doctors trying to resuscitate me.

My chances of survival were slim, and I had been through two major brain surgeries, so it was unclear if I would be the same Paddy Holohan if I ever woke up. The doctors had me on life support and my condition was so severe that they asked my ma if they could turn it off. They insisted that I would end up with permanent disabilities and that I'd spend the rest of my short life in a wheelchair at best. They were worried that I might never be able to talk again. But there wasn't a chance they were turning that machine off, my ma told them. Then, after three weeks in a coma and successive brain surgeries, a miracle happened. I woke up in a hospital bed in a room which was empty, unsurprisingly, except for a nurse, and my first thought was, 'Any ice-cream?' No one could believe it. I had survived. In clashes with death, seven-year-old Paddy Holohan had just notched his first career victory. 1-0.

The doctor, Dr Epcott, saved my life, saved my mobility, saved everything. I died in that hospital, no doubt about it, but I came back swinging, a pattern that would stamp the passport of my life. I wasn't out of the woods yet. I couldn't sit upright for weeks, and if I did, my head would start throbbing and I'd have to lie down again. Stone-throwing was definitely off the agenda, particularly in those first few months post-surgery. Another bump on the head could kill me, the doctors warned, so I had to stay out of harm's way.

The doctors were still running tests but couldn't understand what had caused the clotting issue with my blood. They could see that my body was covered with bruises and jumped to an obvious but incorrect conclusion. I always bruised easily, particularly when playing out on the road, and never thought much of it. I just thought that was the way my body was, but now it's clear that the bruises were caused by my haemophilia, which was undiagnosed at the time. To the doctors, it looked like I was being beaten at home so they called my mam and my aunt and uncle into a room.

'Obviously, this has happened at home and the social workers are now involved. Someone with big hands or fists hit him.'

I was always close to my uncle Paul. He is my mother's brother and looked after me whenever he could. When the doctors tried to insinuate that one of my family members was beating me, he was furious.

'Are you talking about us? Are you talking about me?'

Once the social workers had been informed, I was locked down in the hospital under supervision and wasn't allowed to leave. We were waiting in a room to find out what was going to happen to me when my uncle Paul just said, 'Fuck this,' and picked me up. He hid me in a blanket and ran out the door. I remember sitting on the couch at home eating Coco Pops and thinking, 'I made it.' It was like I had been given a second chance. Not only that, but my aunt Margaret and uncle Paul organised a trip to Disneyland for me to celebrate.

Two years later, I ended up back in Our Lady's Hospital after a simple tooth extraction. It was supposed to be a relatively straightforward procedure but afterwards, my mouth kept filling with clots, almost choking me. One after the other, I physically had to pull them out of my mouth. I would try to sleep but wake up choking, with clots all over the pillow. The doctors had no idea what was going on but it was clear that I was in trouble.

At the time, my ma was busy with my sister, so I didn't get many visits. One visit I will always remember was from my grandad. He hated hospitals and I knew it took a lot for him to come visit me. Some days I'd spend the entire day on my own in the hospital. The doctors continued to run tests but couldn't put their finger on what was causing the clots. I was an impatient nine-year-old and wanted to get out of the hospital. I was sick of being on my own. Luckily, my cousin Roddy visited me one day. He was as wild as I was and just said, 'Let's get the fuck out of here,' and helped me out of my bed. The walk from the hospital in Crumlin to Jobstown was about ten kilometres, a big distance for two young kids, but we just walked straight out the door and headed for home.

We eventually made it to Jobstown, somehow. I'd love to say that my mother was angry with me for leaving, but that wasn't the case. She was happy to see me and confused about how I had gotten out of the hospital, but didn't seem too worried. Even as a nine-year-old, that moment hurt. The newspaper ended up getting wind of my escape and came to interview us. They ran the story with the headline, 'Child (9) Walks Out Of Crumlin Hospital'. The journalist gave me a fiver, and I thought I was getting paid for the story, but looking back now, it was clear he could see that I needed all the help I could get. Not that I cared; we used the money to buy Black Cat bangers and set them off around the estate. The story wasn't all good, though. Once word got around the housing estate, I ended up becoming a target. 'Oh, you think you're smart now being in the paper, do you?' That's just the way it was in Jobstown.

A few weeks later, the doctors still had no idea why I had been clotting so poorly, but they were happy with the improvement I had made. One day a call came through to say that a Canadian doctor had connected the dots and discovered that I was suffering from an extremely rare blood condition, known as Factor XIII deficiency, and that had been causing the inconsistent clotting in my blood. I was the only person in Ireland with this condition and I would need to treat it for the rest of my life. One of the major consequences was that I had a much higher risk of suffering cranial bleeding, so I had to be very careful not to take any bangs or knocks to the head. None of us knew much about Factor XIII, but I didn't care. I was delighted to be heading home.

◆ ◉ ◆

The more we hung around the park in Jobstown and out on the road, the more trouble we found ourselves in with the Gardaí. I still remember the first time I was caught shoplifting and was brought home by the guards. I was nine years old, and my ma said nothing. I found it strange, but I saw it as an opportunity to do whatever I wanted. I knew I could get away with anything.

My aunt Margaret, who lived in Northern Ireland, was the successful one out of the family. My cousin Liam, her son, was a bit older than me and a privileged child. He always had the new Manchester United jerseys, new footballs, little things that all young children get but which seemed alien to me. I was getting his hand-me-downs but it was great because I was still rocking into Jobstown and they were better than most people's clothes.

I loved visiting the North and Margaret's home. Margaret wanted to get me out of Jobstown as often as she could, and I went there every single summer and Christmas from a young age. Spending time in Belfast in a proper family situation brought structure. I wasn't allowed to stay out as long as I wanted, I couldn't tell people to fuck off, and I couldn't break the law. I loved the discipline of it all. It was so new to me. This place, Lenadoon, was just different. I didn't have to worry about all the stuff I was used to in Jobstown. All I had to worry about was swimming, rocking out on the field, playing with the street team, and Northern Irish girls. My aunt Margaret looked after everything and without her, I wouldn't be who I am.

Lenadoon was my escape, but Belfast during the final years of the Troubles was no ordinary place. If I felt that Jobstown was dangerous, it was nothing like Lenadoon Avenue. For my aunt and uncle, Lenadoon was home, but it was also home to one of the deadliest gun battles in Irish history, 'The Battle of Lenadoon', which saw twenty-eight people murdered and

dozens injured during a week of violence in 1972. I thought
it would be an escape from Jobstown, but spending time in
Lenadoon had an impact on my life for ever. Gunshots, killings,
constant fear; Jobstown was a battleground but Belfast was a
war zone.

The fear of life in the heart of Belfast's sectarian violence would
send most children rushing back to Dublin, but for me, the
North had something that Dublin did not: my aunt's husband,
Uncle Liam. In Uncle Liam, I had found a male figure I could
look up to, and someone who truly cared for me. He taught me
about the history of Belfast. I always sought his approval, and
when I found out that he had a blood condition too, I felt extra
close to him.

Margaret and Liam and their family lived in a part of
Lenadoon called Horn Walk and it was a mad place. Lenadoon
was notorious for sectarian incidents between loyalists and
nationalists. My family were from the Catholic side, but coming
up from Dublin, I was caught in the middle. The Catholics used
to call me a 'Free State bastard', and the Protestants would call
me a 'little Taig, a Fenian'. I thought I was hard as nails, battered
and bruised from everything that Jobstown had thrown at me.
If there were guys my cousin was having trouble with and
wanted to avoid, I'd make him show me and I'd run up and
punch them in the face. I had something to prove up there. But
as tough as I thought I was, I soon found out that being tough
in Belfast and being tough in Dublin were two completely
different things.

My earliest memory of the North was one of the scariest. I
was just five years old when I was woken up by the sound of
my door slamming open. Aunt Margaret burst into the room,
grabbed me out of the top bunk and began running through

the house in complete darkness. I had no idea what was going on. The only light in the sitting room came from the street lights outside, and I could make out the silhouette of my relatives on the floor. They weren't screaming but were breathing heavily, lying there with their hands over their heads. Whatever was happening, I could tell it wasn't their first time experiencing it.

Margaret threw herself on top of me, telling me to stay down for my own safety. Pop. Pop. Pop. The gunshots from the street echoed around the room, each one piercing my young ears. We lay in the darkness for an hour and a half while the IRA and the RUC fought their battle outside, but it felt like much longer. Margaret remained remarkably calm throughout, as did my Uncle Liam, and that told its own story. Like so many people in the North at the time, they were used to these incidents, and they had learned to wait for the chaos to pass. My cousins had a routine, lying on the floor to avoid being seen in any windows as you might be mistaken for a sniper. That was how normalised the madness had become. I was used to seeing balaclavas, but five years old, crouched on the floor with a shootout raging outside, that was truly petrifying. I couldn't comprehend the notion that someone could kill me, just like that, without thinking twice.

If Lenadoon was a hotbed of activity, the community centre and the field outside were the epicentre for sure. Activists would antagonise the police and the army, luring them in and then blocking them off with handmade barriers and blockades. A whole field of people, 500 or more, would storm towards them right in front of my house, surrounding the soldiers, peppering them with projectiles. At the time, I was young but had a deep hatred for the British Army. By then, I had seen bad stuff, truly horrific experiences that no young kid should ever have to witness.

There was another night when I was woken up by the sound of screams coming from outside. I looked out and saw a house across the road on fire, and one of our neighbours trapped inside, shouting and banging on his windows. He had fallen asleep on his birthday and the house had gone up in flames. But as the fire started, he ran up the stairs and then couldn't get back down, unable to escape from the inevitable ending. The sound of that moment still haunts me to this day; it wasn't the cries of panic, it was the silence that followed soon after as the flames engulfed the home and swallowed our neighbour up. He burned to death right in front of our eyes. The next day, people were talking about it and I remember my cousin and I wondering what had happened to him. What do you think he felt? What do you reckon burned first? I was about six years old and couldn't quite comprehend what had occurred.

My uncle Paul, who was based in Dublin, travelled a lot between the North and South. We were constantly being searched at the border, and sometimes even taken out of the car, but Paul was cool as a breeze. He'd barely bat an eyelid, would say very little to the border police and wait for them to let us through. I loved those moments in the car, not for the madness but for the thought of having someone close to me who cared about me. Paul was protective of me and was always giving me advice from mistakes that he had made, even though I was too young to understand some of them.

As I got older, some of the riots in Lenadoon thrilled me, to be honest. I looked up to many of the lads in the area, doing everything they could to protect their own people, and would even help to gather stones for them to use during the riots. We always knew when a riot was due to happen because we could see the supplies being stacked up in the estate's alleyways in anticipation. Sometimes it was organised, and sometimes it wasn't. Sometimes it was used to divert attention one way, so something could happen elsewhere. We were young, but we understood the significance of it all. My aunt bate the history into us: the history of Bobby Sands, the history of Ireland, all the way back to Wolfe Tone. I know my history and what it's like to live on both sides of the border. That's why I always wore the tricolour with pride when I was fighting. That's why that part of me exists. It meant so much to me.

One of the worst riots I experienced took place right in front of the house, the army on one side, and the locals on the other. A news crew arrived to try to capture it all. Unfortunately for the cameraman, his camera was forcibly taken and smashed to bits, along with his front teeth. Projectiles of every shape and size were being launched, but things escalated when one of the lads from the estate tried to throw a petrol bomb. Unfortunately for him, he lifted it too far behind and the petrol poured all over his back, setting him on fire. As he rolled around the end of the garden, desperately attempting to put out the flames, the army began to return fire with plastic bullets. Ordinarily, the army would shoot the plastic bullets into the ground and then they would bounce up, but not on this occasion. Instead, they aimed directly at the crowd that had gathered, starting an inverted Mexican wave as people raised their hands and dropped to the floor, looking for any escape.

The riot carried on, getting worse, and it was clear the army and their plastic bullets were responsible for the most damage. There was blood everywhere, and my aunt began helping people into the kitchen, getting them out of sight. We gave out blankets, water, towels, anything we could to help the people who were hurt. There were guys breaking slabs of concrete from the entry, prepping them to be launched. There was an art to this rioting stuff. One group was packing stones, others were collecting bottles, while others searched for petrol and rags. It was like our estate's very own munitions factory and everyone had a role to play in protecting the community.

The violence continued for well over an hour, and darkness began to creep in. Petrol bombs and plastic bullets filled the air, lighting up the night sky like some sort of perverse pyrotechnic show. And then, out of nowhere, we saw the silhouettes of men with machine guns arriving. They looked like heroes. And for a lot of us, they were. It was the boys. The Provisional IRA had arrived.

Back then, the IRA protected our estates from the oppression of the British regime. They looked after all of us when no one else would. They were made out to be terrorists, but a lot of them were just people in the community who came together to stop what was going on, and put an end to the murdering and persecution of their own people. I had experienced the way British soldiers and paratroopers would treat children, their get-the-fuck-out-of-my-way attitude, spitting on us, calling me a ginger cunt. That's where my anger towards them came from.

That particular night, as the riot got worse, a guy came to our front door, holding on to his jaw, with blood spewing out. My aunt tried to help.

'Let me look at it, let me look.'

'Ah no, I'm sweet, I swear to God.'

But he wasn't. When he took his hand away and let go, his jaw dropped towards the floor, exposing the entire inside of his mouth. He tied a sheet around his head to keep it intact and ran out through the back door. That was the last time I saw that man.

Two days later the community held a protest against the use of plastic bullets, and there was a picture of him on a placard. He had died as a result of his injuries. It was in that moment, as I tried to comprehend the incomprehensible, that I realised this truly was a war zone. Any excitement and nervousness that I felt during the riot was born out of naivety, almost as if I felt some of this was a TV show, or a game of Cowboys and Indians. When I stared into the dead man's eyes on that placard, I knew I would never laugh at this violence again. Seeing my neighbour burn alive was not the way I was supposed to experience death. Seeing the man who was shot during his last moments was not the way either. I was too young. For years, I kept a plastic bullet in my house as a reminder; a reminder of just how bad things were back then.

When I went back to Jobstown, I was fighting battles of my own. I was sick of it all, sick of being the brunt of everyone's disillusionment and anger with the world. I was bullied in Dublin and under attack in Belfast. Things got progressively worse until one day, I just said fuck it, I wasn't going to let it happen any more. I was no longer afraid of anything. Why would I be? It was time for the Hooligan, my inner voice, to take over.

I didn't know my ma was dealing with mental health issues when I was growing up, but I was aware that she had her problems and couldn't help me. I knew I was alone from a young age and would have to do my own thing, look after myself. When I was eight years of age, a year after my brain surgery, I wallpapered her bedroom, top to bottom, as I tried to fill the void of being the man of the house.

As time went on, I began encountering the worst types of people, lads that wouldn't give a fuck how old you were, just pure evil, but that was the least of my worries, as an even darker period in my life would begin. I was standing in my granny's house one day, when out of nowhere, my ma walked in and announced, 'I'm getting married.'

'You're fucking getting what?'

I remember it vividly, my mother uttering those words with a sense of pride. And in that moment, she set off a chain of events that would see me enter into some of the worst depression of my life.

It turned out she was getting married to a Nigerian man who she had met recently. As a single mother I always felt she walked around with a cloud of shame hanging over her, and maybe she saw this as a chance to break free from that stereotype. Ireland in the 1990s was a completely different country to the place it has since become, and the pressure the Church put on women led them to feel shameful about pregnancies out of wedlock, something that I know had a huge effect on my ma's mental health.

I could not believe what was happening and I was devastated. My ma was getting married, and not only that, she was getting married to a man I knew nothing about. I was only eleven years old but even at that age, I didn't trust him. There weren't a lot of Nigerians in Ireland at that time, it wasn't as multicultural as it is now, and weddings of this nature were rare. That is until a couple of weeks later when there was another neighbour marrying another Nigerian. Then within a couple of months, there were three or four people getting married, all to Nigerians who were all friends in the same area, as a wave of sham marriages engulfed Jobstown.

'This is a scam,' I screamed at my mother, but she was duped.

'No, I love him, I do.'

I would never accept him as a part of our family. They married quickly while I stood at the registry office, wearing an Adidas jumper, completely uninterested. The situation got even worse when my mother decided to move me out of my bedroom and give it to her new husband. They weren't married a month and already they were sleeping in separate beds. I spent the next two years sleeping on the floor of the landing between the bathroom and my old bedroom with just a sleeping bag and a pillow. My sister was in the big bedroom, my ma was in the back room, and he was in the box room. I didn't even have a bed in my own home. The anxiety that I felt on the streets had turned into a situation where it now also existed in my home. I had nowhere to escape, nowhere that I could truly feel safe. And worst of all, nowhere to cry.

It was around that time that I started dabbling in drugs and drinking heavily, never to the point that I was an addict but I was eleven years old, getting pissed drunk and jumping into robbed cars. I was never one to actually rob the cars, but I had no problem jumping into one that somebody else had stolen or burned out. I always had a good heart and that was down to my grandfather teaching me about morals and pride. Thinking of him, I always felt guilty after doing stupid things.

When the drinking and drug-taking spiralled, I would often fall into the house pissed out of my head and sleep in the hall. I wasn't even a teenager yet, and I thought I was the bomb. Thankfully, we were never taking cocaine, it was just ecstasy and hash. I started to learn how to get money. I could get my hands on anything at that age, and I was always hustling, but I never felt comfortable living like that. I'd do everything I could to make sure no one would ever rip me off, but there were still times when I ended up in trouble. One lad just stood me up against the wall and made me take my runners off, and I did. Afterwards, I made a promise to myself that I wouldn't allow it to happen again. Another time a fella asked me for a smoke and he stepped forward to search me to see if I had anything worth robbing. I just remember smashing him right on the nose, blood spewing everywhere, and thinking, 'I'm not fair game any more.'

As the months passed, my ma's husband and I continued to have war in the house. He offered me thirty quid a week to do chores in the house, which I agreed to, but he never paid me. Eventually, it all came to a head between us and he grabbed me by the throat. I punched him in the head and he threw me to the ground. He had never hit me prior to that because he was afraid of my uncle Paul, but on that particular day, he snapped.

'Right, I'm leaving.'

'Perfect,' I replied. 'That's what we fucking wanted.'

My ma was crying. It was clear she couldn't deal with the whole situation any more. He started to pack his stuff, and then tried to take the television.

'That's my fucking telly. That's ours.'

I went to grab the TV, but he threw it on top of me, slamming me to the floor. My ribs were in bits for weeks. TVs were big yokes back in those days.

I don't remember seeing him again after that. There are times now that I look back and wonder what the fuck my ma was thinking. I was an eleven-year-old kid who was forced out of his bedroom to live on the landing. There was no doubting that I was a little bollocks and a terror to deal with, and I made it a goal of mine to torture this fella. I would cut the soles off his runners, pour ketchup into his pockets, whatever I needed to do. At the end of the day, even though my mother was strong, she was still vulnerable. This was our territory and I was defending it.

CHAPTER 3 ....

I was sitting in my bedroom when I heard the screech of car brakes and a massive bang. I ran out and followed the skid marks over the hill. There it was. A car on the road, upside down. My instinct was to run towards it, but as I got closer, I regretted it instantly.

A trail of human fingers littered the ground. Just fingers, detached from the hand. There was a guy leaning up against the window, gasping for air and I still remember the sounds this poor man was making as he tried to survive the inevitable. It was like a kid sucking on a straw with all their might, trying to get the very last drop of Coca-Cola out of the bottom of a glass. That desperate, failing, sound. I wanted to help him so much, but I just couldn't.

'Are you okay, mate? Are you okay?'

He was smashed against the window, blood pouring out of his ears. Within minutes, the whole estate was circled around the car. I remember stepping backwards away from the crowd, his face imprinted on my memory. I was working a video round for my uncle at the time, renting videos door-to-door, and later that week, we called to a door with a black ribbon on it. It was the house of the man who had died in the crash. That really hit me, to be thirteen years old and so close to death again.

Things at home were getting worse and worse, and I wanted out so badly. I was spending more and more time up North with my aunt Margaret and Uncle Liam. I was being swallowed up by Jobstown, the drink and drugs and the constant feeling of anxiety. I made the decision to move to Belfast. The timing was terrible, however, as Margaret made the decision soon after to sell the house in Lenadoon and move to a lovely little house in Ballinrobe, Mayo. I didn't mind, though; Ballinrobe was still miles away from Jobstown and I was excited about experiencing a new area out west and moving further away from the Troubles up north.

We ended up living in a remote farmhouse, down the back of a lane, behind another house. Despite its isolation, that whole experience was amazing and gave me a new lease of life. There were fields everywhere, sheep running through the meadows, and we even went fishing. It was the freedom I had been yearning for, away from the constant madness of Jobstown and Belfast.

I was always close to my uncle Liam and felt safe around him, almost like he was a father figure. Liam used to drive a black taxi in the North and when he heard about my brain surgery in Beaumont Hospital, he immediately jumped into his car and sped south to get there for me, even breaking through a toll barrier on the way. He was my cousin's dad, my aunt's husband, but I always wondered if he might have been more than that.

By the time we moved to Ballinrobe, my aunt and uncle's marriage was in trouble and came to a difficult end soon afterwards. I was heartbroken and couldn't believe it. Liam had meant so much to me. We eventually moved back to Dublin, and Margaret moved in with my uncle Paul for a year, and he was very good to her. Everyone turned their back on Liam, and I ended up back in Jobstown.

I've heard some crazy stuff over the years, but one thing in particular has stuck with me. My aunt Margaret said to me in a fit of rage one night that Liam could possibly be my father. I was stunned. I couldn't deny that it made some sense, though. He was always so good to me, and, like me, he had a blood disorder too. Even his son, my cousin, the two of us looked like twins. I don't know, though. If it is true and he was around my life and stood back in that manner, he's a coward.

I don't even want to know now. I've passed that stage in my life. I'm raising my own children so I don't need someone to come in and say, 'I missed all those years.' It's thirty years too late. I needed a father when I was in Jobstown. I needed one when I was dying alone in Beaumont. I needed one when I had nothing.

Back in Jobstown, living with my mother, I began falling into trouble. Not serious trouble, but just stuff I did out of boredom. Messing, acting the bollocks basically. My ma wasn't the type to tell me pick up my clothes and we'd always end up in an argument. Even when it came to school she would say, 'Don't go to school if you don't want to go to school.' For me, that was a free pass. When I didn't show up, teachers would threaten to tell my ma and I'd respond with, 'So what? She'll tell you the same thing.' Some of the teachers knew what was going on at home, and when I did turn up, they wouldn't give me a hard time. They could see it, they knew I was struggling.

I can see how easy it is for people to fall into the lifestyle of trying to be a gangster, trying to make money or sell drugs. My gang of friends and I did some things that were illegal, but we never hurt people. The advice my uncle Paul gave me was to never rob from your own. Good or not, that meant something to me. He wasn't involved in drugs; he just ran the video rental business. He used to say 'Holohans get away with nothing, so don't cheat in life.' He was such a clever man and I really looked up to him. He gave me a job working the video round with him, and that really helped me. I realised that I had a bit of charisma, that I was likeable, and it helped to build my confidence back up.

I was making money, legitimately this time, and I was saving it all in the top drawer in my bedroom in Jobstown. On the wall I had a calendar and would mark off different things; if I ate well, if I used the weights in my room, if I had saved money that week. I would put different symbols on different days, and I felt good. I was trying to do well and I felt that I was on the right path, but then things would kick off with my ma again.

Marguerite was going through her own struggles and moved out of the house. She fell pregnant very young, taking the path that a lot of society expects from a working-class teenager. As much as Marguerite annoyed me, I definitely missed her, and being left in the house with just my ma was a volcano of stress that was nearing eruption.

One day, during one of our many fights, we couldn't hack it any more and my ma threw me out. Things had deteriorated to the point where she was calling the police on me for stumbling into the house drunk, and I ended up sleeping rough for a few nights. Sometimes I'd walk to town and roam the streets for the night because I had nowhere to go. I even ran away at one point with my cousin Roddy. We broke into a caravan in north County Dublin and slept there. I was gone for a few days but, like any thirteen-year-old, I missed my ma. I dropped back into

Jobstown in the middle of the night and got back into bed, and nothing was ever said. Not a word. I don't know if I ran away in the hope that someone would show me attention, or whether it was just to escape from it all. Maybe a mix of both, but the attention never came, and that only made things worse.

A couple of months later it got to the stage where my ma was going crazy, and I was getting wild; drinking, smoking hash, rolling in the door drunk. She couldn't take it so she threw me out of the gaff again, this time permanently. I always had this voice within me telling me to get my life together, knowing that I could do better. I never wanted to be the person who brings trouble with them everywhere they go. I just felt like a jigsaw piece in an unsolvable puzzle and nothing ever fitted. I ended up staying with Margaret for a night in her new house in Raheen, another part of Tallaght, and when I woke up the next morning, all of my bags were in the sitting room.

'That's it,' my mam had told Margaret. 'I just can't take him any more. You're going to have to take him.'

I was alone again. Eminem had released the song 'Cleaning Out My Closet' and I remember relating to it, thinking this guy was speaking to me. I felt abandoned, but I began to understand the problems my mother had. 'My ma does love me,' I kept telling myself, 'she's just going through a tough time.'

My aunt Margaret was going through a tough separation herself and everything associated with that, so it ended up with me, her and her sons, Liam and Dan, all living together in this house. I chipped in with thirty quid per week. I had a roof over my head and food in the fridge and that's all I needed. Dan was like my little brother in the house, and I even had my own bedroom. I was given the choice to leave school and get a job, even though I wasn't even fourteen yet, or else stay in school and get things back on track. I was toying with the idea of getting a job when I had a thought that appealed to my competitive instincts. I realised that I would become one of the first Holohans to complete the Leaving Certificate if I stayed in school. My sister didn't complete hers, and my cousin Liam, who was a Henderson, didn't do it. I just kept thinking, 'Imagine if I was the first Holohan to complete the Leaving Cert.' I could show them all. That was enough motivation to keep me in school, and I used the money I had saved from the video round to buy my own uniform and books.

I got my head down and set out on this little mission to turn my life around and prove everyone wrong. I was constantly working out, running, training for something. I didn't know what it was but I made sure I was ready. I was trying to keep myself away from the nonsense that was going on in my own neighbourhood. Some of my other friends decided they didn't want to go down the bad route either and went off to get apprenticeships and became plumbers or carpenters.

Life was good in Raheen, and we were even allowed to have a bottle of beer from time to time. It was a nice environment, almost like a family, but I was still very much an outsider. Sometimes I felt like the adopted child. If Dan wrecked my room, I couldn't say anything about it, or if Liam did something I didn't agree with, it wouldn't be smart of me to voice my opinion. Despite all of that, I was forever grateful because they gave me the shelter I needed at a hugely difficult time in my life. If that hadn't happened, I don't know where I would have ended up, but I'm pretty sure I would have slid off into some sort of darkness where I might not have made it out to tell the tale.

CHAPTER 4 ....

had only moved down the road, but if Jobstown was like a prison, Raheen felt like a retreat. By the time I moved in, my cousin Liam was already a few years ahead of me in school and had made a group of friends. I spent most of my time on the landing doing my weights, out running or doing push-ups. I wasn't working out to look good, I was doing it because I needed something to channel my energy. I probably came across as a real dark, mysterious person, but I got to know Liam's friends and they liked me and became my friends too. For one of the first times in my life, I felt like people actually cared about me, and it felt nice.

Then something crazy happened. Denise, one of the girls in the group, got an eye for me. Margaret's house was one of those where everyone was allowed to come and stay over. It was a nice social environment. All the girls loved her, and she loved company, having people in the house. We were a distraction. She was obviously still going through the devastation of her marriage breakdown and was hurting. At that age, you don't realise these things and it makes me sad that I wasn't able to help her more while I was there. One night when we were all staying there, I whispered something in Denise's ear. I can't remember what I said, but it worked and we began kissing in the hall. I was blown away. I had been with girls before but I'd never had anyone I fancied actually take an interest in me.

Denise had such a different life from me. She came from a good background and I think that was part of the attraction too. Her mother and father were really decent people and embraced me from the start. They knew what I had been through and welcomed me in. The house was nice; it smelled fresh. It was a rare time in my life when I felt truly accepted. I was definitely falling in love and I didn't even realise it. I enjoyed just being somewhere where people liked me and weren't looking at me as if I was going to rob them. It was so new to me. I did everything I could to prove people's stereotypical view of me wrong. Be polite, make your clothes nice, speak correctly. I was always insecure about those things.

I was fourteen, but I was an old fourteen. I was working, sending myself to school, living away from my ma. It wasn't ordinary, and I was still going back every day to feed my dog. I think I enjoyed seeing less of her. Small doses helped and our relationship improved. It was a strange situation to be in at that age, but I was embracing it.

As I started spending more and more time with Denise, Liam and I drifted apart. I was told he liked Denise and that began to drive a wedge between us. It got to a point where our group of friends were no longer just Liam's friends, they were my friends too. There was one moment when I realised Liam wasn't there for me. We were standing on the corner and a big group of guys from my housing estate came around the corner. One of them had just gotten a bad beating by the look of it, and these guys were after somebody. I was leaning on a wall and they started pointing at me. Just as they stepped forward, Liam slipped through a gap and left me there by myself with ten or twelve guys. I was about to get my head beaten in until one of them recognised me and said, 'Oh, that's Paddy. He's from Jobstown, he's sound.' It was a lucky escape, especially considering in Jobstown you often got the punishment even if you hadn't commited the crime, but it taught me that Liam was only out for himself. I confronted him afterwards, but his response told its own story. 'Ah, you know, me ma would have said the same thing. Walk away from trouble if you can.' It made me wonder if I was wrong, but I wasn't. You don't desert anyone in that situation, and I knew my cousin was weak.

Denise and I were boyfriend and girlfriend, but Liam started bouncing from girl to girl. A good friend of ours, Dean Donnelly, had broken up with his girlfriend Tracey after being together for a year. Soon after that, Liam started to see her and began kissing her in front of Dean. I confronted Liam again. 'Ah, you can't help who you fall for,' he said, clearly bullshitting. I knew Dean was upset, but Liam wouldn't stop. It got to the point where Liam and I ended up out the back garden having a knock over it. I'm stubborn, I know I am, and what Liam was doing was wrong, but Margaret took her son's side. That was my eviction, signed, sealed and delivered, and I soon found myself on the way back to Jobstown again.

Going back home made me nervous. My new friends, Denise included, would see what I was brought up in, who I really was. When I told my mother I was moving back in, she just said, 'Okay,' and that was it. I moved back into the back room and started doing up the house. It was as if nothing had changed.

I was always very close to my grandfather as a child, and it was around this time that he got very sick. One day, he took a bad turn. I carried him out of the house with my uncle Paul and put him into an ambulance. I remember crying my eyes out because I knew he would never ever enter that house again. His house was such a safe haven for me. It was a place to visit when things were going badly. I'd run to my granny's and have a cup of tea and escape from it all. I'd watch wrestling with my granddad and it felt like a portal to a happier life. It was just us and we were safe there. He was the one solid man in my life, but his Parkinson's disease got worse and he was in hospital for about a year before he died. My uncle Paul and I would go up there every single day to look after him, clean his feet, clean around his mouth, go to my granny's, deliver the smokes. If my own son looked after me the same way that Paul looked after his father, I would die a happy man.

The day before my granddad died, the two of us were alone together one last time. He had gangrene and it caused a burning sensation that really affected him. 'Patrick, my toes are burning, Patrick,' he would say in distress. And then he called out, 'Andy, Andy,' waving at the end of the bed. I didn't have a clue who Andy was and I went home and asked my ma.

'Andrew?' she said. 'He was Granddad's friend that was killed in the Congo.'

My grandad had told me the story from his time when he was in the UN forces in the Congo. Andy, his friend, was only out there so that he could earn enough money to buy a wheelchair for his disabled kid, and he had been killed with an arrow through his eye. My grandad took his body, tied his hands and legs to each other and carried him back to camp. He told me how he carried Andy like a school bag and ran for miles, like a jungle version of Forrest Gump. Now, here my granddad was, at the end of his life, screaming for his friend, and I could see on his face how it nearly gave him energy.

When he died the next day, I lost a huge part of my life. Every man takes something from different men, but they only have one father. I didn't have a father. At different times in my life, different people have assumed the role and been part of the overall jigsaw: my uncle Paul, my uncle Liam, John Kavanagh in later years, and even my aunt Margaret, but before them it was my granddad. Those people guided me and shaped me. I followed their goodness, their pride, their legacy. And when one of them passed away or was no longer in my life, it hurt badly. It was like losing a father every time.

I remember burying my grandfather on 1 October 2003. I was fifteen and Denise, who supported me so much through it all, was standing there with me. I couldn't look at anyone at the funeral, I just kept crying. I was trying so hard not to cry, but the more I held it in, the worse it got. I threw a rose into the grave and made a promise: 'I'm going to do everything I can to fulfil what you stand for. Being proud, being present, looking after your family.'

The next year of my life was blank. A year of nothing, just a numb feeling of emptiness trying to get over the passing of my granddad. I tried to settle back into life in Jobstown. I was still in school, and I was working as hard as I could on the DVD round with my uncle, saving every month. I even took a few shifts working on building sites. Some days I didn't go to school, but that didn't mean I wasn't getting an education. I learned more in a week on those sites than I ever did in school.

I eventually saved enough money and at seventeen, I bought my first car, an Opel Corsa, and started doing deliveries in the chipper as well. I was a grafter, making €150 a night, two nights a week, in the chipper, on top of the €120 I was making for the DVD round. Every way I could, I made money. I paid €5,000 for my first insurance policy on the Corsa, more than the car was worth. I was delighted with myself, but I could see my teachers looking at me and thinking I was a drug dealer. I wasn't. I won't say that there wasn't a time when a box of bogey runners or jumpers would fall into my hands and I'd sell them, but I was a hustler and I was doing whatever I could to make a few quid.

A few months later, my uncle Paul offered me his Opel Astra. An absolute belter of a thing, it had neon lights under it, custom body kit, and it was like something straight out of the Fast & Furious films. There was a couple of grand's worth of repairs to be done but Paul said it was mine if I fixed it. I remember thinking, 'This thing is an animal. I'm going to be the bomb in this yoke.' Once I had it fixed up, I started driving to school, parking wherever I wanted. My car was better than what half of the teachers were driving, and that made me feel even better about myself, but it didn't last too long.

I headed off on a road trip with two of my mates, Adam and Robin, to Arranmore Island off the coast of Donegal. We drove up in the Astra, but when we got up there, something happened and it broke down. I thought it would be fine to leave it by the pier but when I came back to it later, the locals were after stripping the car to bits; they took the bumper and all. I set off on a rampage, and in the middle of the night, we ended up fighting a group of the islanders. I eventually got some of the parts back and towed the car back to Dublin. I remember looking at it sitting outside the house in Jobstown, bits littered all over the garden. I was gutted. Naked. I left as a cool motherfucker with a whopper car, and I came back with it on the back of a truck, dismantled to pieces. Before I could get it back on the road, someone burned it out. It broke down and I parked it in the wrong estate. When I came back, the car was on fire.

I felt like I was doing well for myself, but when it came to my relationship with Denise, I was acting like a bit of a shithead. We were on and off, and I was becoming a bit of a 'Jack the lad', but we were young and foolish. Every time I wasn't with her, though, I always missed her. But I was young and I became afraid that I was going to be with the same person for the rest of my life. I think I just needed a break.

And then I met Lola. She had caught my eye a few times, and she was a little bit younger, but I fancied her to bits. She was a stunner. If the sun touched her skin, she would tan immediately. I was amazed when it turned out that she liked me too. 'I thought you were out of my league,' she said, and there I was, this little skinny ginger lad who couldn't believe his luck. I had a bit of a reputation in the area because I had a car, a job, and all that, but I still didn't see myself in the way that she saw me. I'm friends with her older brother now, but we nearly had a knock when he first heard I was dating her. I told him that I wasn't there to mess around and that I just wanted to be with her.

Lola had been through her own troubles before I knew her, but she was doing okay when we met. She couldn't drink alcohol. If she did, she would turn into a completely different person. The two of us ended up really clicking, but I was stupid and young. One day I would feel like I was in love with Lola, and the next it would be Denise. I ended up sleeping with Denise behind Lola's back.

I was lying in bed one day when Denise stormed into my house in tears.

'I'm pregnant.'

I was in shock, but I put my arms around Denise and told her, 'You will not get a better father than me.' I was weirdly happy about the idea of being a father. I wanted to have a family. I wanted to have what I didn't have growing up. I didn't want my son to go through what I went through.

When I went to meet Lola, I went with the intention of telling her everything, but I bottled it. I told her I had slept with Denise, but couldn't bring myself to tell her about the pregnancy. She was devastated, absolutely devastated. It broke my heart just saying those words. I had never felt guilt like that. It ate away at me. When I told her about the pregnancy a few days later, she was floored.

It was around this time as well that a friend of mine, Israel — Izzy — went up to a bridge in Blessington and took his own life. We were heartbroken. We just couldn't understand it. That was Izzy, though. He did things his own way and didn't care what people thought of him. I guarantee he didn't even stutter from leaving his house all the way to the bridge. I just wish he would have shared his troubles with those closest to him.

Months later, we went to a benefit night in Izzy's memory which meant that both Lola and Denise, who was heavily pregnant by that time, would be in the same building. I spent the night sitting with Denise, but I knew how uncomfortable that would be for Lola, and I was going mad inside. There was nothing I could do, and when Denise was leaving, I left too. She went home and I stopped off in the local nightclub called Level Four, or, as we knew it, 'Sticky Floor'.

The next day, Lola rang me in tears. I could hear how upset she was as soon as I answered the phone.

'I need to talk to you, I need to talk to you, Paddy. I was with a young fella last night, we went home together, I didn't want to be with him.'

'Tell me who it is, tell me who it is,' I screamed down the phone.

'I can't, I can't, Paddy. I can't.'

The next day Lola finally told me everything. She had been sexually assaulted by someone close to me, someone I once would have considered a friend. I went out looking for him immediately, but he was nowhere to be seen so I turned up at his mother's front door. The minute I saw his face, I knew it was him. I couldn't even say anything, I just started throwing punches and couldn't stop. Blind anger. His ma came out and pulled me away, but I jumped into my car and drove home.

The Gardaí got involved after that. Lola made a statement, and then they rang me to make one too. To this day, I haven't spoken a word to him. Myself and Lola drifted even further apart as well. I don't think she ever recovered from what happened that night.

I needed help. I had lost a mate to suicide, lost a girlfriend, and I was really struggling. I went to speak to the school priest, Father Martin, and told him what was going on in my head, all of the really dark stuff. I wasn't religious, I just needed someone who I could talk to, and Father Martin was there for me when I needed him most. We still speak today. He knows I'm spiritual and helps me, a guiding light. The first time I went to talk to him, I latched on to the fact that I was about to become a father, and how I'd see things differently once the baby was born.

'It's all sorted, it's all solved now, Father Martin.'

He looked at me in shock. I could see he was genuinely concerned for me.

Inside, I knew he wouldn't understand what I was feeling. Once I became a father, I wouldn't need anything else in my life. If I could help that child become a better person than I was, and give him or her a good life, that was the only thing in the world that would matter to me.

A few months later, Denise went into the hospital for a routine appointment, and the doctors discovered that her blood pressure was too high. They needed to deliver the baby right away. We were brought in and Denise went into labour. I was scared shitless, a fresh eighteen-year-old with no clue of what to do. Hours passed, the clock spinning around in circles.

And then it happened. The nurse handed me our baby boy, and I burst into floods of tears. Because of my haemophilia, the hospital had found out early about the baby's gender, and expected a girl, but the doctors had got it wrong. I held our new little boy, Tiernan, and a surge of confidence overcame my body. I wrapped him up and made a promise to him right there and then.

'I'll never leave you, son. I'll do everything I can to make sure that we make it.'

CHAPTER 5 ....

When I was young, defending yourself was part of the Jobstown survival pack. Being able to box or to fight was a necessity. There was no better way to stop people from hitting you than to let them see you hitting someone else.

I knew absolutely nothing about martial arts and the UFC. I didn't even know different martial arts existed. I had bounced through karate, boxing and kickboxing lessons from the age of seven. I was a month here, a month there, but I never stuck with any of them. I was obsessed with Jean-Claude Van Damme, Bruce Lee and Arnold Schwarzenegger. Even Jackie Chan — I loved the fact that he did his own stunts. I played football as well when I was young and for most of my limited career, I was a little terror, a vicious right back. Fighting came naturally to me, though, on the pitch as well as off. Sometimes you'd turn up for a game of football, but end up throwing down.

My uncle Paul gave me tips on how to look after myself and what to do when I did get into a fight. One thing he told me was to wave my hands up and down, to make the other person stutter, and then land a right hook. I loved the idea of fighting and not just the one-on-one aspect. I loved the aftermath of it and the buzz. I loved replaying every moment and thinking it lasted for ever when, in truth, most fights only last for seconds. They fly by in the blink of an eye. Fighting fascinated me.

When Denise was pregnant, I didn't want to end up as an average joe hanging around the estate. I wanted a bit more meaning in my life. Little did I know that walking into an old building in Rathcoole would change my life for ever. Dean Donnelly was a close friend of mine, and he and his dad Jim were always trying different sports and classes, so I'd follow them. Jim tried powerlifting once but I knew straight away it wasn't for me. Lifting things that didn't need to be lifted? If I wanted to do that, I would have just started a furniture removal company. At least that way I would have been getting paid.

One day, Dean asked if I would like to try this thing, jiu-jitsu, in a gym in Rathcoole with the two of them. I didn't even know what jiu-jitsu was. Jim had started training and Dean was going down with him. 'You're not getting better at fighting than me,' I told Dean, and that mentality dragged me through the doors of Straight Blast Gym for the first time. I expected to see this big, imposing figure with an intimidating attitude running the place, but I didn't. A softly spoken, kind, polite guy came over and shook my hand.

'I'm John Kavanagh.'

If you had asked people what SBG was back then, they wouldn't have had a clue. The entire organisation was very much in its infancy. John had earned his black belt in jiu-jitsu earlier that year, and his was the only SBG gym of its kind in Ireland. In fact, along with one in Manchester and one in Estonia, these were the only SBG gyms outside America at the time.

There was an aura around John. I could tell instantly that he knew what he was doing, where he was going and the road that we needed to take. He was clearly enjoying what he was doing and it was a pleasure to be around him. There was a crazy Icelandic guy walking around the gym in his pants with a blue belt on: John's good friend, and an absolute phenom, Gunnar Nelson. Gunni looked scary but was incredibly polite, like most Icelandic fighters I know; dangerous by reputation, but so kind in nature.

John was never a vocal coach. He was a man of few words, and very to the point. He would teach the class, and I would eat every single word of his. If he told me to go home and chase chickens because it would make me better, I would have, no gloves needed. There were times in the early days where he put his weight on me on the mat and that's when I knew the world had changed. It was no longer the case that someone could beat you up just because they were bigger than you. When John went chest-to-chest with me on the mat, I felt like I could not breathe. It was pure positioning, learned over years of practice and an understanding of how to distribute your weight to your advantage. It was like being smothered by a wet blanket. It was eye-opening and blew my mind.

John was living in Rathcoole with his fiancée at the time and came from a lovely family. I remember looking at his life and thinking, 'That's what I want. This is where I need to be.' This was the raft that I had been looking for, and I was going to hold on to it until it took me where I needed to be. Classes took place on Tuesdays and Thursdays and I was obsessed from the beginning. We used to listen to a workout tape by Bas Rutten, the renowned mixed martial artist — 'Jab, Cross, Uppercut, Defend' — and my goal was to be fit enough to beat that tape. After a few weeks, I turned to Dean.

'I'm going to do this for the rest of my life.'

I became more and more confident in my own ability, but one moment knocked me down a few pegs. There was a boxing sparring session one Thursday evening and I was just after finishing a class upstairs.

'Can I jump in? Can I jump in?' I begged John. 'I can box.'

'Yeah, go on in,' he said.

This was John's seal of approval and a great confidence boost for me. He was giving me that pass because he knew I was ready for the next stage — or so I thought. I threw on my big gloves and jumped in.

I was sparring a few guys, and then it came to a smaller girl. Aisling Daly must've been about five foot tall with pink hair. I didn't expect much. We touched gloves and I decided I'd take it easy on her, but I soon learned that was a big mistake. She obliterated me, just lit me up from the first second to the last. I carried myself back to the car afterwards and wanted the world to swallow me up. All of the passion and excitement that I had before had been smashed to pieces. My pride dented, I didn't know if martial arts was for me anymore. Maybe I was wasting my time.

That was when I realised that martial arts was totally different from anything I had done before. It was like the Matrix. The focus was no longer on being bigger or stronger; it was about knowledge and experience. It was a journey. Try again. Fail again. I was left with a choice: either run away or come back for more. I chose the latter and the feeling of worthlessness lasted a day before I was itching to get back to the gym again. I knew Ais was good, but now I knew how good she really was. It was the last time I'd underestimate her. My humbling at the hands of Aisling would eventually have a hugely positive effect on my career.

Starting out, I wasn't trying to be a UFC fighter, or trying to make it professionally. I was just trying to be in a better place with my mental health. I had so much stress in my life and I had finally found something to help me deal with that. When I was in that gym, I felt a high that I had never felt before, not with anything legal. Being there was like finding another wave of father figures. John assumed that role and SBG, that little gym, became my family. I wanted to belong, and I knew that this place would take my life in the direction I needed to go. All I needed was to be loyal and hard-working, and I had both characteristics in abundance.

The mentality and culture that John created was so motivating. It was an environment where it was okay to learn and it was okay to lose. The gym was a laboratory, and we were the rats. Trial and error was always the order of the day. It wasn't about being the toughest, it was about learning and effort, and I found that addictive. The quote 'Tough is not how you act, it's how you train' was right there on the gym wall. Effort, shortcomings, failings; that was my language. That was the story of my life rolled into one big ecosystem. I always failed, but it always made me better. From the moment I met John, I felt that jiu-jitsu could get the best out of me as a person. I put my faith and hope in it and John.

At that time, there was something very special going on with SBG. The people involved were the best martial artists in the country, the top dogs, and if they said something, you listened. I became a model student. John had grown up in Rathfarnham, a nice area, and I was probably one of those lads he tried to stay away from when he was growing up, but he had seen it all before. Owen Roddy was the same as me. He was from Ballymun, another young pup bursting with enthusiasm, and had been brought over to John by a friend of his. The story goes that Roddy got into a fight at a chipper van, and a guy knocked him clean out with a kick to the head. A few days later, Roddy went back to the same fella, asking him how he did that with the kick. He was angry, but he was like me. He wanted to learn.

Martial arts in Ireland was in its infancy in those days, and it wasn't as easy to access information as it is now. Information was key and John was a sharer. He shared everything. If John caught you with a guillotine, you would have to saw your chin off to get out of it. There were times I used to look up at him from the mats, and I was in awe of his ability. Obviously, the feelings weren't reciprocated at the start — I was just one of the guys in the beginner class in the gym — but as time went on, I earned his respect a little bit by turning up on time and working hard. I had a vicious triangle from the start, I'd catch a giraffe in it, and I knew John saw something in me. I never became cocky, though, and that was a result of the environment John created. That mentality, that was his.

Aisling became a close training partner of mine. I respected Ais from the moment she started pummelling me on my first day, and now that John was my coach, Ais could tell me things that I would never ask him myself. In reality, I didn't really know John outside the gym. Where did he come from? Was he religious? All of these things. As time went by, the vision I had of John was a magical one. He was this strong man who had everything together and was going to guide me, going to push me to the heights I was capable of getting to. John knew the answers before I ever had to ask the questions. Even in my early fights, I would tell John, 'You take the controller.' This jiu-jitsu stuff was witchcraft. I was trying it on guys and they were turning me upside down and strangling me in ways I never even knew. Boys, girls, big, small, wide, tall. Being in SBG, it was like I had uncovered a secret that nobody else knew about. John was the master Splinter and we were his Teenage Mutant Ninja Turtles.

To me, loyalty is when someone can remember the times you helped them when you had nothing to gain yourself. I remember doing crazy little things that you would never catch a UFC fighter doing for his trainer. One time, John's sister, Ann, was feeling claustrophobic and anxious in her office. I'm a dab hand at wallpapering and I went in one Sunday and wallpapered the whole place as a surprise. Little stuff like that, making Ann feel a bit better, was making John's life a little easier and that's what I wanted. If we're a family, I'm all in. If you need me to teach classes week in week out, open the gym early in the mornings, I'll do it. I'm extremely loyal, but sometimes, my loyalty goes too far.

One night there was a new arrival in the gym, a young lad in boxing shorts who had been dragged up to us by either his dad or his boxing coach. I took little notice of Conor McGregor at first, but as we were warming up, I glanced over and was immediately struck by how quick his hands were. I was definitely taking notice now, and so was everyone else in the gym. I saw myself as a bit more of a grappler than a boxer, but Conor had that mean attitude, that aggressive chip on his shoulder. Behind it all, you could still see that little twinkle of excitement in his eye. He was a student of the arts and wanted to learn. I started about eight months before Conor, so I was still relatively new, but Conor and I had a similar energy and we connected right from the beginning.

Word started to go around the gym about a move from Rathcoole to a new gym facility on the Long Mile Road, and I remember being so upset when I heard.

'I'm not going to be able to travel to the gym, it's further away.'

That was just an excuse. When we moved, there was real excitement. The Long Mile gym was just special. It was the place that gave birth to some of Ireland's biggest MMA stars. Our character was forged there. When we went to that gym, I soon got over the extra commute and fell in love with it immediately. There were day sessions on, and I got the opportunity to start teaching classes myself. I used to go to a class at 6pm and then I would coach the class after that. I wasn't paid for coaching those classes but I didn't care at the time. I was just delighted to be seen as a coach.

The new gym felt like a palace compared to Rathcoole, with a huge mat and a wall, but the story goes that when John first went to see the building, it was so run down there was even a tree growing in the middle of it. Unwanted foliage aside, the gym represented progression. I had learned a lot of the tricks of the carpentry trade and spent time on building sites so I was there to give John a hand as much as I could. It took effort from everybody, pulling mats, buying tarps, to get the place built and ready to open. Jim Donnelly was building the gym, the dressing rooms, fixing toilets, everything, and we helped him as best we could. It felt like we each played a part in building our new home. I still have the big brass key for the Long Mile Road gym. Anyone who had a key knew what it meant to have one: early starts and late finishes.

John was sailing the ship and he was the captain, but I was learning from all of the crew as well. As time moved on, I got to know everyone in the gym. Mick 'Sissy Boy' Leonard was famous for falling out of the ring back in the day and knocking himself out off a table. I remember seeing him on a poster in the dressing room and being mesmerised by the fact that I was training next to him. People like him felt like celebrities. I even remember bringing one of my close childhood friends, Robin Powell, up to train, and I regretted it immediately. I felt like SBG was my secret. I didn't want anybody else to have it.

It was in the Long Mile gym that I earned my blue belt in jiu-jitsu. There were over fifty people there on the day of the grading. Matt Thornton, President of SBG at the time, flew over from the US to give a seminar. He turned up at the gym, this big seven-foot guy, the guy that I had expected John to look like when I first walked into the Rathcoole gym. Matt taught us about the idea of aliveness training, the idea of the basics being the most important, leaving the spinning kicks at home. He had figured that out and when he passed it on, it made a lot of sense.

Other clubs were allowed to grade with us and travelled from all over the country. The Irish martial arts community was a tight-knit group back then, and these were the golden years to me. Everyone was together. This was at the time that if someone had a brown belt, they could fucking levitate, and it was unheard of for a guy to have a purple belt. There was one black belt in the whole of Ireland and that was John Kavanagh, but he was soon followed by Andy Ryan, another top-level coach. I came out for my grading and performed well, nailing an arm drag takedown on my opponent. Matt turned to John and said, 'Where did he learn that?' Of course, I could only have learned it from one man: my coach.

When it came to calling out the belts, I was positive that I wasn't getting one. Back in those days, a blue belt was earned and not bought. A blue belt to me was a god among men. When Matt called out my name, I was shocked. Me, Paddy Holohan, a blue belt in jiu-jitsu. Jim Donnelly got his blue belt too and no one else. Of the fifty people, it was just the two of us. If I needed any proof of how far I'd come in a few short years, this was it. Sometimes, experiencing pain can change everything. I had felt enough pain in life to know that I needed to keep on going.

Round 2

CHAPTER 6 ·····································

Jiu-jitsu made me whole. It made me feel like I was part of something positive, and it had a huge effect on my mental health. I started out fighting in the MMA League on the amateur circuit. We'd turn up, register with a piece of paper, pay our entry fee, fight three fights on a mat in a community hall on the same day, and we'd do it four times a year. It was basic, but I enjoyed it. At the same time, myself and Denise both got places on a FÁS course called Sportech, which was run out of Tallaght Leisure Centre near the top of my road. I can still remember the feeling I got when the letter finally came through the door to confirm my place on the course, jumping for joy. Life was heading in the right direction.

I felt good about myself and excited about the future. I was performing well on the amateur circuit. I made it to the final of the MMA League in my second year but I was disqualified in the first round. Without even thinking, I jabbed my opponent in the mouth, which wasn't allowed, and Clive Staunton, the referee, waved the fight off. Still, I always felt like I was a level above my opponents, even if I didn't look it. John sensed that too, no doubt, and he approached me one night in the gym. It was one of those real steamy nights, when everyone was working hard and you could see the hot air rising from the mats. He punched me in the arm.

'Do you want a fight?'

I didn't understand what he meant, I thought he wanted to fight me, to be honest.

'I've got a guy,' John explained. 'He's from Galway. He has a guy fighting out of his club and wants you to fight him.'

I agreed to it instantly. I remember going outside the gym, standing next to my Mitsubishi Lancer, and ringing Denise.

'John is after asking me to fight. I made it, I finally have a professional fight.'

John had a show coming up called Cage of Truth. It used to be called Ring of Truth, but things were improving and we had a cage now. It was in the Good Counsel GAA Club and Conor, who was 2-0, was the main event. Conor had knocked guys out in the Ring of Truth before and now he had the chance to do it right on his own doorstep in Dublin 12. The idea of how good he was, even at that early stage, was something I just could not wrap my head around. It was ridiculous.

I grabbed my opportunity like a triangle choke, and there was no way I was letting go. I trained my socks off, running the hill in Killinarden Park, a place that would become a central part of all my camps. I used to visualise my opponent on the top of that hill in my head and run towards him. I'd sprint it thirty times, hail, rain or snow, while my mate Adam timed me. I'd grab a gas canister and throw it over the goalposts. It was proper old-school training, but I knew no different. I had a point to prove to myself. I didn't want to be an ordinary guy. When I was dropping Tiernan to school, I wanted people to say, 'That's Paddy Holohan.'

The day of the weigh-in rolled round and we were upstairs in our 'dressing room', a little wooden shower room on the Long Mile Road. Conor was there along with his opponent, Artemij Sitenkov, and a few others. The things that Conor says and does, people think it's all an act, but it's not. Conor started to mean-mug Sitenkov across this tiny room but Sitenkov, who looked like a Lithuanian Bond villain, just smiled and laughed. His coach was there too and began to laugh as well, but that only annoyed Conor further. He turned around immediately and eyeballed Sitenkov's coach.

'Do you fucking want it? Do ya? I'll bring you downstairs now and you can fucking get it, and then he'll get it in the cage tomorrow as well.'

That was the birth of the famous, 'If one of us goes to war, we all go to war.' If it came down to it, I was there to back Conor up and he would do the same for me. It was the SBG way. My fight weight was 148lb, and when I eventually stood up on the scales, I was 139lb soaking wet — and that was after a curry the night before as well. Myself and John never discussed money for the fight. Even though I was broke the money wasn't of huge importance to me; I was just happy to be finally fighting my first professional fight.

When fight day came round, I was nervous, but I was ready. It felt like I was going to fight someone on my housing estate rather than someone in a cage. I jumped on the Luas and headed for Good Counsel. Looking out the window at the people passing, I felt like I was in my own Rocky film. Everyone was going somewhere else, living their daily lives, and I was on my way to fight a man in a cage, not knowing what awaited me on the other side. I walked straight in the doors of the club and up to the table where Ann, John's sister, was working. I was just about to say my name when I was interrupted by a massive Galway lad with a thick country accent.

'I'm here to fight Paddy Holohan,' he said.

'You're fucking what? How could you be fighting me? You're a lump of a lad, what does your ma be feedin' ye?'

We nearly had a knock at the table right there and then, but I headed for the dressing room, and shut the door. Fuck, I knew I was in for a tough night.

The crowd started filing in. All my friends and family were there. It was the first fight my mother went to, and it was also the last. It just wasn't for her. Dean's younger brother, Scott, was there and he made a poster that I still have today that said 'Go Paddy, Go!' This was the top of the world to all of us.

Finally, it was time to go. Owen Roddy was taking my corner. Owen was a legend in the game, a man who would decapitate his opponent with a knee. I knew I was in safe hands. I pulled up my grey hoodie, which had 'Tough is not how you act, tough is how you train' printed on the back. It cost me €50 but it felt like armour when I had it on. As soon as I opened the dressing room door, I could hear the music playing, and I ran. Ran through the crowd, ran into this little cage, ran around the side of it. This would turn out to be one of my trademarks, running around the cage, but that first night, I just did it out of pure aggression and pent-up frustration.

The fight turned out to be a slobberknocker. This guy, Shane Bane, was good and caught me with a few clean shots. It was a mad situation, I didn't even know the rules. Sometimes shots were going to the head, other times elbows and knees were being thrown.

'Go for an underhook,' Owen shouted, and I just responded, 'I don't even know what an underhook is, man.'

All I knew was that I was in a standup war and there was no way I was going down without a fight. I could hear everything from inside the cage, which made it hard to focus. My ma and my family ended up sitting on the wrong side of the cage, which meant they were near Bane's supporters, who were screaming, 'Kill him, son!' and my ma was screaming, 'Stop fucking saying that!'

At the start of the second round, I took three consecutive right hands to the face. My inner voice was saying, 'Move, move,' but I couldn't. I just ate the shots. I finally snapped out of it, moved out of the way, and we ended up rolling around on the ground. Once we touched the canvas, I knew there was only going to be one outcome; that triangle was going to go jingle-jangle. I stuffed one of his hands, got in the triangle choke, and he tapped out immediately. The place went crazy. I had done it. Done it in front of my friends, my family, all of those who mattered to me most. My mother was on the opposite side of the cage and I tried to jump over and touch her hand.

The post-fight madness eventually quietened down, and I jumped back on the Luas home to get dressed to go out. My ear was swollen, my face was banged up, but I had a little metal plaque in my hand with 'Cage of Truth' on it, my trophy. Everyone was asking me what it was for, and that feeling of pure achievement was simply amazing. When the Luas pulled up to Tallaght, I was so exhausted that I couldn't walk. Both my legs were dead and I had to ring one of my friends to collect me and spin me home. I didn't care, though, as long as I had my first professional trophy riding shotgun with me. The celebrations started with a few drinks in my house before we headed into town to a nightclub called Redz. The whole gym was there that night. We got a lock-in until around 8am, followed by a breakfast roll in the shop. We sat outside as the sun came up, me, Dean, John, Ais, and a friend from another gym, Stephen Lowry. The birds were chirping, and life started to seep into town. I was covered in cuts and bruises, without a penny in my pocket, but it was probably one of the happiest times I've ever experienced. For me, I was exactly where I was supposed to be.

Paddy Holohan, 1-0 — July 2007

I didn't know it at the time but it would be nearly three years before I was back in the MMA cage again.

I loved my year on the Sportech course. Denise and I were qualifying at the same time and she was incredible, somehow managing to balance everything that was going on. She was young, and she was going through her own difficulties, but she was always the perfect mother to my son.

When I finished up with Sportech, Mick Browne, the guy who was in charge of the course, put my name forward for an opportunity to travel over to Canada. Living in Vancouver, staying with a French-Canadian family, was a completely new experience for me. I got a job as a fitness instructor in Vancouver Technical Secondary School, where I was running spin classes, aerobics, even jiu-jitsu. I was training in jiu-jitsu as well in the Gracie Barra gym on Broadway, and I wanted to test myself. I put my name down for the British Columbian Open tournament, which happened to fall on the same day as Tiernan's second birthday. I won gold in my division, but standing on the SkyTrain home afterwards, I felt completely alone. The crippling knot in my stomach that I woke up with every morning was homesickness, and I couldn't shake it. I made a promise to myself, that I would see out the rest of my time in Canada, but that when I got home, I was going to make it as a professional fighter.

I couldn't wait to be home in Ireland and to have Tiernan there with me again. I came home even more hungry to learn and develop than ever before. I went back to my job in the chipper doing deliveries, and trained like a madman at night. I was running, swimming, practising jiu-jitsu. There was a second floor in the gym now, and I was leading a jiu-jitsu class from 6pm to 7pm downstairs while Conor had his own class upstairs from 7pm to 8pm teaching boxing.

At the time, we were like two spotty teenagers, but Conor's striking classes were some of the best I've ever experienced. His classes were always high-intensity, making us really graft in those sessions. He would put us on rotation and set the timer in his head. Two-minute rounds could quickly turn to nine-minute rounds. Some of the sessions were as tough as anything — one look at the blood on the canvas and you knew it could tell some stories — but afterwards, there was always mutual respect. That was the SBG mentality.

Conor caught me with a left hand one night and broke my nose. It was a round that started off as a little bit of a spar but became competitive. Neither of us wanted to give the other an inch. Conor appreciated moments like that when I was giving it back to him. That showed real respect. We finished a round, and the bell rang in the gym signalling the end of the class. I glanced at Conor and he nodded back, 'Let's do another one.'

I wasn't going to back down, so we ended up going again. He gave me three consecutive left hands to the face, with the third one doing the damage. I told myself, 'Move! Move!', but he was just too fast. I remember the sheer power from that left hand.

Boom.

Boom.

Boom.

'Fuck, Conor. You're after breaking my nose!' To this day, my left nostril doesn't work.

When Conor taught classes, he broke his lessons down with intense detail, similar to John Kavanagh's grappling sessions, only in stand-up. Conor showed us that it wasn't about hitting the pads for ten years or smashing a bag. It had to be surgical and technical and you needed an understanding of what to do when the shots were coming. I still teach some of the stuff I learned from Conor during that time. My mentality as the smaller fella was always 'Live, survive, keep going.' It didn't bother me that I wasn't hitting as hard as the likes of Conor, Owen Roddy or Keith Coady. Keith was a training partner of mine who had a punch like a donkey's kick. I knew jiu-jitsu was my strength. I was always trying to get to the clinch. I remember John saying to me, 'You're my jiu-jitsu guy, Paddy.' Hearing those words from someone like John made me feel so great.

That was the heyday, putting our blood, sweat, tears and fears into the sessions. We literally and metaphorically built that gym, physically laying down the slabs that people were walking on. We all felt like we owned a part of SBG. Jim Donnelly put that gym together with us as his apprentices. One summer,

Conor and Jim built a second floor in the gym. Years later in training, Conor would scream, 'We built this didn't we, Jim!' Smashing the bag. 'We put this fucking floor together!'

While all of this was going on, another opportunity presented itself. Owen Roddy was sparring Chris Fields and injured his elbow while trying to block a kick. Roddy was set to travel to France to fight a guy named Mickael Daboville. Daboville was one scary dude, but John came up to me in the gym.

'I have a fight for you. Do you want to fight in France?'

I was delighted. This was what I had been training for, and I was ready to get back competing again. It had been nearly three years and in the meantime, I had gotten my qualifications, but I was still flat broke.

'John, I don't have any money,' I reminded him. 'How am I going to get to bleedin' France?'

John laughed as he told me that I would be getting paid for the fight. I couldn't believe it. €400 plus travel expenses — I felt like a millionaire. But when I saw a video of Daboville, I immediately regretted watching it. Daboville walked out against Rob Quinn — 'Rob The Dawg' — who was the top lad in Ireland at the time, and punched him in the face. Rob ended up doing a backflip, and getting absolutely mauled. Rob was training in the gym with us and I turned to him.

'Any tips?' I asked, looking for some little bit of hope.

'Yeah,' he told me. 'Don't get hit.'

Coming from a guy who had once fought two brothers on the same night, Rob's advice didn't exactly fill me with confidence.

Going out to France, I knew that if there was one fight where there was a chance of me getting knocked out, this was it, but if Daboville was going to beat me, he was going to have to kill me. Three weeks out, Cathal Pendred gave me some simple advice.

'Paddy, just fucking train your bollocks off for those three weeks and go for it.'

So that's what I did. I ran every day, sometimes even twice a day, up to twenty kilometres. John didn't come to France with me, as he had arranged a camp in Portugal, and I felt like I was on my own in that regard, but I couldn't use that as an excuse. Clive Staunton, the referee who had disqualified me a few years earlier in the MMA League final, headed out with me instead to do my corner. Clive was one of the old-school lads in Irish MMA who paved the way for the rest of us as much as anyone else. This fight against Daboville was the start of my journey, and he was there for me. Years later, when I walked out at UFC Dublin on the biggest night of my career, I made sure that Clive was in my corner again.

We flew out to Marseille and I was expecting to see this beautiful French city, but the city was more like a doormat than a postcard. There were prostitutes and gangs on the street, and it was difficult to feel at ease in that environment. Valentijn Overeem, whose brother Alistair would go on to be one of the top UFC heavyweights, was also fighting on the same card and we ended up clicking from the start. We were outside the hotel one morning and Valentijn said to me, 'I have the flu so I need to get this fight finished quickly.' I couldn't believe his attitude towards winning. He wouldn't let the flu stop him getting what he wanted and I admired that outlook. And sure enough, seven seconds in, he tagged his opponent a few times and then stiffed him with a head kick. Knocked. Out. Cold.

I was nervous on the morning of the weigh-in, even though I was well under the limit. I was 138lb full of breakfast for a 145lb fight. Ciaran Maher, an SBG teammate, was fighting on the same card and he needed to cut weight. I remember him shouting from the hotel bathroom, 'If I shower, do you reckon my body would absorb water?' I laughed, but I didn't have a clue really. Our knowledge in those areas was still so basic.

The weigh-in was in French, and I could barely speak English, so when it was time for the staredown, I just stared at Daboville and tried to look deep into his soul. He smiled right back at me, the pasty, ginger Irishman with the broken posture and in the old Dunnes Stores boxers, and clearly thought he had this fight in the bag. My mentality was always the same: come home with your shield or on your shield. I remember one time Conor said to me, 'You don't realise how good you are. You don't know.' And it was true, I never put much thought into how good I actually was. I just knew fighting was in my genes and I would never be afraid to throw down.

When fight day arrived, the nerves increased, but I was ready, sharp. I was in the warm-up room and I remember seeing a guy asleep in the corner and wondering how the fuck he could be so relaxed before fighting someone. I was puzzled. 'It's the dangerous ones that sleep, Paddy,' Clive said to me, and he was right. Later on, the Russian woke from his slumber, completed a few stretching exercises, walked into the octagon and annihilated his opponent with ease. I knew I was in a different battlefield from Good Counsel GAA Club then. Everything about the setup — flags, dancers, a pre-fight parade — it was all next-level stuff. We had all the food we could want. I ate every cake I could get my hands on, a little kid from a council estate let loose on this feast. On the outside, I was aware of representing the country well, but on the inside, I was thinking, 'Take everything you can.'

When the time came to make my walk, I was still nervous, but I was able to channel it in a positive manner. I was pacing in circles, talking to myself. 'I've got Tallaght behind me,' I told myself. 'I've got Ireland behind me. I'm an Irish warrior.' Ten beautiful girls in tartan skirts came in, and I soon realised they were my dancers for the ring-walk. Not the best preparation for a young red-blooded teenager trying to get ready for a fight, but I did my best to stay focused. I walked up the steps and appeared out of the ground in the arena, into a crowd roaring and baying for blood. I don't know why, but it happened again; I ran down the ramp as quickly as I could and into the ring. As I was running, I looked up and saw an Irish flag at the top of the roof. Someone had climbed all the way up there and planted that flag for me, and more than ever, I had to do everything in my power to win. It was no longer Paddy Holohan versus Mickael Daboville. This was Ireland versus France.

When the first round began, my inexperience in terms of my striking was obvious immediately. We exchanged shots but Daboville was on top, landing some big hits. John had told me before I flew over that he had no ground game.

'Dirt on the ground, he's dirt, Paddy,' John assured me. 'But his standup is good, so stay safe.'

Daboville caught me with a strong right hand and I remember this lightning sharp out-of-body experience. 'No, I've been knocked out, it's over.' And then all of a sudden, I was back. I ate the shot, but I was still there. The fact that I was still standing gave me a real lift and it propelled me forward. We ended up grappling eventually and I got Daboville to the ground. I had him in a foot lock, but it didn't work. My leg was caught on him inside an inverted heel hook position, so I decided to bail on the foot lock and try to stand up, but my foot was stuck. I was driving through his guard, trying to kill him, but my leg popped out somehow and I ended up past his guard.

I got an Americana armlock on the far side of side control and his head was still trapped in the loop. This was perfect. I knew what was coming next. I stood up, pulled Daboville back into a triangle, and choked him out cold. His body went limp, and it gave me energy. This monster thought he was going to come out here and beat me, but it didn't work like that. The pride and adrenalin ran through my body. It wasn't about fame. It wasn't about money. It was just pure emotion. Clenching the Irish flag, I was now 2-0.

Beating Daboville made me realise that my mindset was perfect. It wasn't Paddy Holohan these guys were fighting. Whether they knew it or not, they were up against the Hooligan. I think John actually came up with the nickname, Paddy 'the Hooligan' Holohan. I was always known as 'Hoolo' around the road, and sometimes people would say 'Hooligan', so it was always there, but it was John who really brought it to the mainstream. It's tough to truly explain what this alter ego is. I expected the Hooligan to turn up at the door before my fights, and he did. This 'fuck you' mentality creeps into my body and consumes my thoughts. He talks to me, just like when I was younger and going through some difficult times out on the street. That never-back-down attitude that I needed to get through life. It's the Hooligan in my head that helps me to gather every ounce of my being and keep driving forward, regardless of the circumstances. There was no way I would ever step back, no fear.

The realisation of the danger that I was potentially in that night didn't really hit me until a few months later. Chris Fields was fighting up in Strabane and after he weighed in, we all went for a meal together: Chris, John, myself and a few others. In front of the whole table, John turned around and said, 'To be honest, Paddy, when you were going out to fight that lad in France, I thought you were either going to submit him, or else you were going to get really hurt.' Everyone at the table laughed, everyone except me. I had a two-year-old at home and putting myself in serious danger was not something to laugh about. The gloss of the win quickly wore off once he had said that. It was a serious situation, and his words struck me harder than any punch from Daboville.

As we were leaving the stadium in France that night, Valentijn Overeem got handed an envelope. It was bursting from the seams with cash. He was only in the ring for around seven seconds and got paid over a grand for each one. Immediately, I told myself, 'That's fighting, that's where I want to be. I don't want to be feeling these fears, risking everything, without being reimbursed.' With one glance at that envelope, and the smile on Valentijn's face, my mindset changed. It was time to stop these fights for a couple of hundred euro here and there. I was working hard. I needed to get paid.

I was paid €400 for beating Daboville, and Ciaran got €300 for his fight on the same card so I gave him €50 and we both made out with the same amount. The next day, we woke up after a blurry night to the news that every flight out of the country had been cancelled. The Icelandic ash cloud was bringing air travel worldwide to a standstill. Ciaran's plan was to stay on for another week due to the lack of flights, but I needed to get back to Tiernan so I began to plot my way home with Clive.

We got dropped to the train station at Marseille and got a train to Le Havre, in the north, where we booked into a hotel for the night. €200 each later, I was already down to €150 out of my fight purse. The next morning, we had to force our way on to a packed ferry, which took care of another €100. Less than forty-eight hours after my fight, I had €50 to show for it and we still weren't home because the only ferry available brought us to Portsmouth in England. We still needed to get a train to Holyhead and then one last ferry to Dublin. That last €50 didn't go very far and I'll always be grateful to Clive, who paid the €200 for me to get home.

When we finally got home, I gave Tiernan €50, even though he wasn't three years old yet and it was technically Clive's money. I had just beaten a guy who no one had expected me to beat, and best of all, I did it in his own backyard. I had nothing but a win, a limp from my sore knee and an empty pocket. But to be honest, I didn't even care. I was back in Dublin and had my son in my arms.

Paddy Holohan, 2-0 — April 2010

CHAPTER 7 ··

My career was heading in the right direction, but one foolish moment threatened to derail everything before it had really even started.

I was in Wexford one night visiting my mate Robin, who was in college there, and a lad came up to me on the dancefloor and said, 'We don't like your type around here.' I was shocked, it was totally out of left field, but no way was I backing down.

'Fuck you,' I retorted and smiled back at him. As this happened, his mate ran in from the side to hit me, but I was too quick and moved out of the way. He left his arm there, so I caught it and we ended up rolling over. I did everything I could to try to break his arm, but the bouncers got there first and dragged us all outside. It carried on out there. The little ginger fucker from Dublin wasn't going to be allowed to make a fool of the big Wexford lad, and his friends came around the corner looking for their revenge on me. They came at me again and I ended up catching one of them with two or three slaps before he rushed me against a shutter. I ended up on the ground and caught him in a foot lock, in the middle of a Wexford street, the ultimate embarrassment, and the guy ended up squealing in pain. The Gardaí arrived and there I was holding on to this lad's foot for dear life.

'I'm not letting go of this oaf until you have a hold of him,' I told them. My side of the story fell on deaf ears. The guards dragged me towards the van and, despite me protesting my innocence, they put me in cuffs and threw me into the back along with the guy I was fighting. So there we were, sitting opposite each other, cuffed in the back of a Garda van, and round three kicked off. I just started loafing him across the seat and the two of us had a go at each other all the way to the station. It was like *Dumb and Dumber* with the dogs in the back of Harry's van. We were destroyed when we reached the station, but the Gardaí didn't care. Meanwhile, my friend Robin had ended up in a scrap of his own and he ended up being brought to the same station, so now the two of us were in cells in a Wexford Garda station. Two Dublin lads in a cell in Wexford on the same night, for two completely different incidents; you can certainly take the lads out of Tallaght, but you can't take Tallaght out of the lads.

That night set off a chain of events that would see me end up in court and nearly lose my chance of ever competing in the UFC. The Gardaí said I was a competitive athlete and it was assault with a deadly skill. My solicitor was doing everything he could to prevent me from getting any charges, telling them that I would need to travel for my career and that the UFC would never touch me if I had a record. Despite that I ended up getting charged, and then found guilty, on everything.

I was dragged down to Wexford for months at a time, going to various hearings, court date after court date, putting myself up in accommodation. It cost a lot of money, something that I certainly didn't have at the time. Instead of community service and probation, my solicitor told me that if I appealed I could end up facing a prison sentence. I appealed the decision anyway in a last-ditch attempt to clear my name and save my career, but I knew my chances were slim. When the date of the appeal finally arrived, it was set for Dublin city centre. I got the Luas in and turned up at court fearing the worst. I had taken the Luas to many battles, and I knew this would be my toughest, until something strange happened. The day of the appeal turned out to be the same day that Her Majesty the Queen was coming to Ireland on a state visit, and when I arrived in court, there was barely a guard to be seen. The judge stood up, wrote everything off, and my name was cleared. After the 800 years of hardship, I suppose that day the Queen wasn't so bad after all.

Another bullet dodged. Paddy Holohan — still undefeated.

After beating Mickael Daboville in France, I was training even harder, going all-in on my journey to become a professional mixed martial artist. The Irish MMA scene was buzzing, with events north and south of the border and gyms sprouting up all over the country. I beat Richie Ivory from Arklow in my next event, but after fighting in a stadium in France, it felt like a step back to be in some GAA club again. Once that had been taken care of, I was booked for a card in the National Basketball Arena, just down the road from where I grew up. It seemed as big as Old Trafford to me when I was younger, and it became the Colosseum of Irish MMA before the big nights in the Helix and the 3Arena existed. It was a moment I had always dreamed of, the lad from Tallaght fighting in front of a home crowd.

Fight night finally arrived and I was nervous. I could hear the whole of my road outside the dressing room, expecting victory and nothing less. This was my opportunity to finally become a hometown hero. I had visualised the moment with every sprint up the hill in Killinarden, and now it was time to deliver. The weigh-in the previous day was the first time I'd seen my opponent, Milan Kovach, in person and I was taken aback by the sheer size of him. He was significantly bigger than me and looked like he cut his own hair, which is always a sign of a dangerous man. All I could do was laugh.

Running out into the arena, I soaked up every ounce of the energy, the venom. I took one look at my corner, at Dean, at Ais and at John, and then I touched gloves with Kovach and the fight was on. He threw a head kick at me straight away, but he underestimated my speed and I avoided it, almost in slow motion. My mind was in complete control. I bided my time, waited for the right moment, and then shot for the takedown. Bang. Just like that, he was caught in the web.

In those moments, I don't even have to think, I just savour them. The Hooligan takes over. My hands were always moving, but I wasn't the one controlling them. I was a spectator, floating my way to 4-0. He shrank in size, a shadow of the man at the weigh-in. I could smell the fear, his eyes reminding me of the dark chapters of my youth, afraid, broken, alone. I knew in his head he didn't expect to feel like that. I heard the clapper — bang, bang, bang — telling me I had ten seconds left in the round. To everyone outside the cage, I was running out of time, but I had my man right where I wanted him. I locked in the rear naked choke fully and Kovach tapped with one second left on the clock.

The arena erupted. I puffed out my cheeks and stuck it to every single one of them.

'I told you, I told you all. Never underestimate me!'

I used to savour these moments, take in the success, and try not to rush back to life straight away. Take thirty seconds to enjoy the euphoria of what I had achieved. I grabbed the microphone and let the people know that I was no different from any of them.

'I'm nothing special,' I told them. 'I'm one of you. Just a kid from Jobstown that put my mind on something and here I am. If I can do it, then you can do it too.'

That Kovach fight taught me a lot about myself, but it also taught my friends a lot about me and just how good I really was. Later that night in the club, I remember Macker, a childhood friend of mine, saying to me, 'When he first came out, I thought you were fucked, but I'm telling ya now, you better drink this pint as my apology.' I was on such a high, I couldn't get drunk. Even at 6am the next morning, I was back in Jobstown, lying in my bed, playing the fight back in my head and still thinking about every punch, every roll. My obsession with my sport was getting deeper and deeper. I had put together a plan. Now it was finally starting to come together.

Paddy Holohan, 4-0 — July 2010

My next win came in December at the aptly named 'The Fight Before Christmas' against Andreas Lovbrand. Lovbrand was flying in from Sweden, so I knew he meant business. He was a purple belt in jiu-jitsu, and there weren't too many around at the time. He was dangerous, a submission specialist, and he already had beaten Neil Seery, one of the toughest northsiders you could ever meet, but I was still confident I could beat him. The fight was still in the first round when I faked a jab right hand, and unleashed the sharpest, hardest head kick I'd ever thrown in my life. Smack. I caught him flush on the chin. His bottom teeth flew through the air and onto the canvas. By the time my leg reached the ground, an explosion of blood and teeth had covered the two of us. I scurried to the other side of the cage and unloaded a flying knee, but Lovbrand caught it and dunked me on my head. It would have been a spectacular finish, but now I was in a lot of trouble.

I ended up on the bottom and I trapped his hand with my legs, holding the other arm so he couldn't elbow me. He was stuck and knew I was going to try a submission. I moved so that Lovbrand's head was on his arm, stuck between my legs, in a triangle position from bottom side control, but that was just a decoy. I wanted him to think that's what I was going for. Keeping him in a reverse triangle from bottom side control, I reached over with my right hand and caught an Americana on his arm. I couldn't believe it; I was about to land this crazy submission that I'd been working on in the gym. As I pulled his hand back, it felt like I was breaking a chicken wing. Lovbrand let it go and his shoulder imploded. Crack. Tap. Tap. Tap.

I got paid €150 for that win and I picked up the €50 'Submission of the Night' bonus as well. I drove to the fight in the thickest of snowstorms, got the win, and drove home. That was the reality of things back then. I was driving home afterwards with the lads in the car — a Mitsubishi Lancer at the time — still high on adrenalin, buzzing after my win, when the lights started flashing in my rear-view mirror. The Gardaí. I was used to being pulled over, but the timing of this one could not have been worse. I was covered in scratches and I still had Lovbrand's blood on me because there were no showers at that arena. It looked terrible.

The guards whipped me out of the car and stood me up against the bonnet. In the space of an hour, I went from being a hometown hero in front of a full GAA club to just another scumbag in the eyes of the Gardaí being searched in the middle of Dublin.

'Do you have a licence? Identification? What's all that blood from?'

I told them that I was a professional fighter, that I had been fighting that night, but at the time MMA was still largely unknown.

'Is it like karate?' they asked me. 'What is it?'

Had I said cage-fighting they probably would have known straight away, but I couldn't let those words leave my mouth.

'It's martial arts in an arena.'

'Well, you've no identification and you're covered in blood so you'll have to come with us,' they insisted.

I was furious, but then I remembered something. 'Hold on!' I ran to the boot, took out a half-ripped piece of A4 paper from my gear bag.

'There, look,' I showed them. 'It's the poster from the fight.'

It was in black and white, but clear as day, the colourful mug of Paddy Holohan was on the front. The guard laughed when he saw it.

'You're some mad fucker, do you know that? I definitely thought you were lying. I was dying to hear the real story. Go on so, off you go.'

Covered in blood, €200 in my pocket, and a black-and-white poster with my face on it. Times were good, but the money still wasn't. I was fighting UFC-level guys for KFC-level wages, and something had to change.

Paddy Holohan, 5-0 — December 2010

After beating Lovbrand, I pretty much went straight back into a training camp for my next fight. I was booked for an event in Derry called Chaos where I'd be in for a tough night against an experienced opponent, Neil McGuigan. McGuigan was a member of the Police Service of Northern Ireland, and the thought of that brought me back to being a little kid in Belfast and witnessing the death and destruction that these men caused. It made me angry, the angriest I had ever been before a fight. I wanted to destroy Neil McGuigan.

That training camp felt different, and I couldn't understand why. I didn't spar one round, and maybe I was becoming complacent or allowing other things in life to take up space in my head. I was more angry than motivated, and I think I was just worn out. Maybe it would have been wiser to take a break after fighting Lovbrand. I wasn't experienced enough to notice these things at that time, but I was mentally drained. I should have taken six months to chill, and come back hungry. Instead I was cruising, and that's dangerous. You need to be rough. You need to truly want it. You need to be sharp.

We drove to Derry, carloads of us over the back mountain roads. When I got into the cage, I felt a bit loose, but not in a positive way. As the first exchange happened, I could hear John shouting at me straight away, 'Relax, relax!', and I knew that I was trying too hard, overthinking things. I was trying to kill McGuigan, and being emotionally driven is a dangerous way to fight. My mistakes cost me and I got rushed and taken down. While I was on the bottom, he hit me with an elbow that snapped me out of my lull. 'Fuck, it's on now,' I thought to myself.

I managed to gain guard, stuffed his hand and I caught him in a triangle. There were four minutes left in the round; this was how it was supposed to go. I kept tightening and tightening, but it didn't feel right, he was supposed to be asleep by now. There were times I could hear him choking and struggling for air, but he still wouldn't tap. My legs started to fatigue, but there was no way I was letting go of the triangle. I kept squeezing and squeezing, landing elbows on his head, waiting for him to go limp, but it was no use. He hung on. He kept pinning my head with one hand and tagging me with the other, doing everything he could to reach the bell. And when the bell went, my opportunity went with it. I had spent so much energy on that one move, chasing the finish, and it was a struggle just to get back on my feet. My legs felt like cement.

The second round started with a few exchanges before I got the upper hand and caught McGuigan in another triangle. Again, I couldn't finish. He was a tough fucker. I was physically shattered, and worry about the third round began to set in. My mindset changed from attack to survival, with everything resting on the final round. My legs were becoming heavier with every second. Every attempt to remain standing was a struggle. I was two rounds ahead, but that mattered fuck all in my current state. It was just about seeing the fight through. I landed some shots, he landed some shots. We were both tired, and ended up against the fence, taking turns at taking each other down. Somehow I ended up catching him in a guillotine and began trying to pull his head. Conor was sitting in the front row and

I could just see him screaming.

'Pull! Pull on it, Paddy! Elbow back! Pull on it!' I looked Conor dead in the eye and shouted, 'It's not working, it's not fucking working.'

The bell finally tolled and the fight was over. I was exhausted and, even if we were up North with a northern referee and two northern judges, I had dominated for three rounds. I had done enough to earn the decision, and a unanimous one at that. We stood in the middle, and I could feel my hand being raised, but then I looked over and could see his being raised too.

'What the fuck?!'

I couldn't believe it. Somehow the judges had scored the fight a draw. I thought it was a pathetic decision. I was putting my life on the line, and then this amateur shit ruined everything. I felt anyone looking at the fight would see it was a clear win in my favour. I had no doubt they fucked me over that day. But I respected Neil after our fight and the anger I had towards him disappeared. He was just a normal bloke like me. We went back to the dressing room and I collapsed onto the floor, lying on the mat, oxygen deprived. I was getting sick, and I felt like I could genuinely die. John, to be fair to him, still decided to show me how to finish the triangle properly and I'll never forget that lesson. I would not make the same mistake again.

I felt so screwed over after driving all the way up there. Jason McCabe, the promoter, came up to me in the cage right after the fight and handed me a cheque for £500. I had no idea what I was going to be paid. There was no situation where John would sit us down and tell us the game plan, how it was going to go, work the pads with us, reassure us, hug us. No pep talks, it was never like that. It was a case of us turning up to the sessions and classes in the gym and then, 'I'll see ya in Derry.' It worked, but it definitely wasn't the fairy-tale situation where people think that it was like a Mickey and Rocky relationship. It wasn't like that. John as a technical coach, being able to break things down, was incredible. When it came to showing you the mistakes you were making and how to avoid them the next time, he was a genius, but from the human and emotional side, he wasn't as strong.

'The result was a disgrace. Can we do anything?' I asked him. 'Is there anything that can be said, John?' But his reply was concise.

'Jason McCabe isn't like that,' he said. 'I don't think he would be the type of guy to screw you over. I don't think it was a draw but I can't do anything.' I didn't blame Jason, but I thought those judges definitely fucked me over.

John should have fought my corner for me that night. He should have tried something to right that wrong, but he didn't.

'It's over, Paddy,' he told me. 'Just forget it.'

But it wasn't over. It was a stain on my record forever. And if anybody asked, I told them I had won.

Paddy Holohan, 6-0 (sort of) — February 2011

CHAPTER 8 ....

I didn't have to wait long to set the record straight against Neil McGuigan. I was back fighting in the National Basketball Arena within a couple of weeks, and although I was disappointed with my performance against Steve McCombe, who was fighting for the thirtieth time as a professional, I still won by unanimous decision. After that, I was booked for a rematch against McGuigan — back up to Derry for Chaos 9. This time the training camp went well, a mixture of determination and fury driving me forward each day. The minute I entered the arena, I knew McGuigan didn't stand a chance. I steamrollered him and won by rear naked choke in the first, taking my record to 7-0 (and one draw), and officially shutting the door on any question marks people had about who was the better fighter.

I was in the car driving home afterwards when the phone rang. It was John, asking me if I wanted to fight in a bantamweight Grand Prix.

'The guys in it are Rob McCrum, Artemij Sitenkov, Damien Rooney, and Paul McVeigh,' he told me.

My first instinct was that I was fucking exhausted, but I couldn't miss out on this opportunity. I knew that if I got through, I'd be the number one guy in Europe and Ireland. I finally had the potential to turn my career into something I could be proud of for ever. I had to take it. I was on the way home from one fight and already I had booked another three. I knew an extended rest was definitely out of the question, so I took a few days off, spent them with Tiernan, and got back into training. I was nervous and excited, but I was ready to go to war.

I was never really into the party scene whereby I would win a fight and party for ages. There were sessions and shenanigans, of course, but I wasn't one of these people who couldn't wait to get back to the barstool. For me, it was more about not being blinkered by the idea of one fight. I just wanted to be able to eat what I wanted, to have a life back for a few days because I had given mine to MMA. While everyone else was doing normal things, I was in this state of anxiety because I was going to fight someone and they were training to hurt me. I spent a year or two feeling like this, fight anxiety, and although I could feel myself getting better at dealing with it, I still found it difficult. It was around this time as well that I started to realise my own potential. 'You're fucking good at this, Paddy. Believe in yourself. This is something you can do, this can take you to where you need to be.' That idea of being a hometown hero, being able to show my son what I was achieving, it spurred me on.

I was drawn to face Damien Rooney for my first fight in the Grand Prix. Damien was a step up in opponent — at the time, he was out training in the US with top-level guys — and an all-out war was expected, one where even the fans were anxious. The fight was set for the King's Hall in Belfast and, finally, I was heading home. The weigh-in was in Curley's, a shopping centre where I had spent many hours as a kid, stalking the teddy bear machine, hoping the claw would fish out a £20 note when I had used up my only pound. When we got to the weigh-in, I walked past that machine and it was like I was walking past my childhood. I could see myself, reminding me just how far that kid had come.

I was excited to fight at the King's Hall, one of Belfast's most iconic venues. As I was getting ready in the dressing room, I could feel a little tingle in my back. It was the first time I'd felt it but I know now that my body was worn down and trying to send me a signal about the damage I was putting it through. It's difficult to decipher the difference between pain and injury in that pre-fight tension, particularly when the panic and nerves are trying to take over. I was always good at absorbing the nerves and using them positively. It's like being at the top of a rollercoaster and you don't want it to go over the hill, but you know it's going to happen anyway. As it drops, you're not thinking, 'Ah shit, this is horrible.' You embrace the giddiness and that release of adrenaline. I used to just accept that there would be some fear and doubt, so I'd march to the cage and lock them inside the door with me.

Right before fights, my head was always like a glass of fizzy orange, popping every few seconds. John was great in these moments because I would ask countless questions and his responses would have a calming influence on me. Having someone backstage screaming, 'We're going to kill him' would never have worked for me. I needed someone to pop with me, moving around to my pace.

I caught a lot of people off guard that night, Damien included. I had made my name as a submission artist, but in the build-up to the fight, I had been working with a lot of good strikers, including Conor and Owen Roddy. I was confident in my hands, moving Damien around the ring. I knew he was going to try to shoot and take me down, but I was ready for it. As he made his move, I caught him flush on the face with my knee.

It sounded like an A4 hardback slapping off a wooden floor. BANG. I fell at the same time but leapt straight back up and moved in to finish the job. Damien lay flat on the floor and as I was about to land that final shot on him, his eyes caught me dead and stopped me in my tracks. His sockets were as empty as an unlocked car in Jobstown, nothing left. His arms lay stiff by his side, his jaw locked. Damien Rooney was out cold.

In that moment, I thought I had killed my opponent and all sorts of negative thoughts entered my mind. The ref stopped the fight and my team jumped into the cage. I celebrated for a second, but then snapped out of it, remembering Damien's situation. I felt so bad. He was seriously hurt and had to be lifted up from the floor by his coach. When I looked at Damien, that's when I told myself, I never want to be there. I never want to be in that situation.

When Damien had been helped out of the cage, I could finally allow myself to celebrate.

'Paddy Holohan, how did you do that?' the interviewer asked.

My reply was simple. 'Because I got the skills. I'm not here to mess around. I'm here for the long run.'

The following week, I went to a bar in the Abberley Court Hotel to watch my fight against Damien Rooney on television. The promotion, Cage Contender, had a deal with Setanta Sports which meant the cards were shown a week later. The only other time one of my fights had been on TV, I was away on a stag, and this time, nothing was going to stop me from watching my fight. When I went into the pub, there were a few lads sitting at a table in front of the TV.

'Is there any chance I could sit at that table? Because I'm trying to see the telly behind you,' I asked them. The lad turned around and bluntly refused. I remember thinking, 'Ya little prick', and walking to the other side of the pub, feeling embarrassed. The fight came on and I had a crick in my neck trying to see the screen from a horrible angle so that I could get a glimpse of my moment of fame. Before long, the group of lads spotted that it was me fighting on the screen.

'Come on over and sit beside us, I didn't realise.'

'Go fuck yourself,' I shouted back across the room. The fight came on, I knocked Damien Rooney clean out and with that, the expression on the lad's face changed dramatically.

Even to this day, I still struggle with preconceived expectations people have of me because I'm from Jobstown and I wear a tracksuit. I was going to do a TV show in Dublin in late 2018, and the taxi that was sent for me refused to pick me up outside my house without paying cash up front, purely because of where I was from. It got to the point where I had to order a different taxi. Despite the fact that he had to drive past a twenty-foot mural of me to even get to my housing estate, this driver still had his issues with collecting me.

I've dealt with discrimination all my life but I'm proud of where I am from, and things like that make me want to change people's perception of my hometown even more. I'm from Jobstown. My nickname is 'the Hooligan'. I look like a scumbag, I'm told, even if I don't know what a scumbag is supposed to look like. Yes, I wear a tracksuit and runners, but where I come from a tracksuit is exactly that — a suit.

Paddy Holohan, 8-0 — April 2012

The reward for beating Damien Rooney was a fight against Artemij Sitenkov. Sitenkov had already fought and beaten Rob McCrum and Neil Seery in the Grand Prix, and he had a victory against Conor on his record from their fight back in 2008. I knew I was going up a level. He wasn't aggressive-looking or intimidating, and that was the scariest thing. Given the chance, he could snap your leg off. The fight was going to be a puzzle and one that would put me in serious danger if I failed to solve it.

The fact that he had beaten Conor was even more motivation. I could still remember the anti-climax after Conor lost that night. To me it felt like, 'How fucking dare you take that away from one of my mates? I'm going to get you for what you did on that night.' If they fought again ten times, Conor would knock him out each time. But Sitenkov was like a Chinese finger-trap, he would lure you in and gobble you up. It was just one of those nights. It was bigger than just Paddy Holohan vs Artemij Sitenkov. We all wanted to get this guy.

Trying to break down the fight, trying to solve the puzzle, kept me awake at night. People might think that John shared tape with me of fights and broke them down that way, but that wasn't the way we operated. He was more hands on the mats. Sitkenov's fights always went by the same playbook; immediate overhook, wade through the shots and wrap up the leg on the same side, then roll over onto the shoulder, grab the opponent's leg and snatch them. In training, John showed me a move that when he wrapped up his leg, I needed to step beside his standing leg and block it. I'd then be able to push him forward, forcing him to just fall over. It was so simple. Obviously I would have to be careful that I blocked Sitenkov's leg, but John told me to keep on practising. I drilled it hundreds of times each day in preparation for that fight, knowing I would get an opportunity to surprise him with that move. I believed in my process: staying elbow to elbow, wrist control, turning my heel in, turning my heel out, being careful and understanding the other side of heel hooks and knee bars.

At the time, leg locks were frowned upon. If you jumped on someone's legs, it meant you didn't know what you were doing. We all know now how ill-judged that perception was, but that was the mindset back then. It was borne from a lack of knowledge more than anything, because we simply didn't know enough about that aspect of martial arts back then. There was one guy with us, Pavel, who was a purple belt at the time, and he helped me a lot with preparation because he was foot locking everybody. My good friend Kamil Rutkowski had a mean foot lock too, so he helped me with my training. I was eating up every crumb of material, falling asleep watching an online webinar every single night. I became obsessed. All my thoughts were consumed by it, and continue to be, even when I'm in bed at night. I can't stop thinking about new ways to win.

One Monday night, a few weeks before the fight, John set the rest of the gym a challenge while we were training.

'If any of you can foot lock Paddy, I'm willing to give you a free month's membership in the gym and a T-shirt,' he announced.

At first, I laughed it off and thought it could be fun, but the situation actually started to get a little dangerous. A month's membership was a lot of money, considering none of us had any. The entire gym was out to get me and I was under constant attack. There were times when I was walking around the car park, packing my stuff into the boot of my car, and people would dive at my legs out of nowhere. It was intense, to say the least, but I kept swatting them away like flies. Even Conor, the last person I would have expected a foot lock from at that time, grabbed my foot one night. He looked me dead in the eye and tried to snap my leg off. He tightened the grip with every passing second, trying harder and harder to make me tap. My foot was about to break, but I just couldn't give him the satisfaction.

'I'm not fucking tapping, not tonight.'

I was going through this process of fighting the entire gym, preparing to fight one of the best leg lockers in Europe, when an unexpected guest showed up at the gym: Artemij Sitenkov's coach, the very same coach Conor got into aggro with a few years earlier. I immediately thought that he was there to find out as much information as possible from my camp, but John allowed him to stay and train with us.

'He's not with Sitenkov any more,' he told me. 'We could learn from him.'

It was John's gym, so if he wanted him to stay, there was nothing I could do, even if it did make me feel uncomfortable. I remained suspicious but just kept training.

'I'm not with Artemij anymore,' Sitenkov's coach tried to assure me. 'You're going to beat him. He doesn't train. This is why we don't get on any more. He has that leg lock and that's it.'

Whatever about his motives for being there, I didn't like the way he sold Sitenkov out, but I took my opportunity and got him to show me some defensive moves. I knew that if I could get past that leg lock, Sitenkov would break.

The camp went well and my feet stayed foot lock free, somehow. On the last day of camp Conor and I were sparring rounds and I was in awe at the manner in which he was able to take the form of my opponent; walking, talking, moving around the gym just like Sitenkov. Trying to roll under my leg, attempting to catch me, it was like Sitenkov himself was with me. I was defending everything and doing really well, but it was the measure of Conor that he only ever wanted me to do well and would do everything to help his team. Some fighters revel in other people's downfalls, but not Conor. He wasn't like that. Some fighters wouldn't like to see their teammate beat someone who had a win over them, that toxic mentality exists in gyms, but with Conor, it's all of us or none of us.

When fight night came, I got ready to drive to the stadium but found myself nervously sitting in my car. Leaving the house, I looked my mother dead in the eye and told her, 'If I come back and my leg is broken, don't be worried about me.' Not that it mattered though, my ma never worried about anything. There were times I was heading off to fight and she would just be like, 'Okay, see you later.' But this time was different.

'What do you mean?' she asked me.

'This guy doesn't really attack you, Ma,' I tried to explain. 'He just snaps your leg in pieces, but don't be worried, I'll be fine.'

I don't even know why I had that conversation with my mother, I guess it was just to speak to someone in the hope that it would relieve the stress and nervousness building up inside my head. Even on my journey to the stadium, I couldn't get the idea of Sitenkov breaking my leg out of my head. Every few seconds I took my eyes off the road and looked down at my legs pressing the pedals. If I lost and Sitenkov broke my leg, people wouldn't even be able to see it happening, such is the speed and skill involved in a leg lock. It's like one rare spider within a ball of spiders; you just can't spot it through the madness.

With each negative thought, doubt and fear grabbed me again. I had to get out of that mindset quickly, there was too much at stake. Instead of pulling in, I turned onto the M50 motorway, dropped a gear and just let it rip down the road. For the next twenty minutes, I zipped up and down that motorway at speeds of over 100mph.

'Crash, Paddy. Just crash and let it all blow apart. Bow out now.'

But then the Hooligan took the wheel. 'Fuck this, drive straight to the stadium. Ride the buzz and go straight from the car park into the cage.'

That was probably one of the best things I've ever done before a fight, because it gave me an adrenaline rush like no other at a time when I needed it. The fight was in Tallaght, my town. If I had to live the rest of my life with my leg inside out just to get a win that night, then so be it. Not only that, but I had this little tiny thing in the back of my head, telling me that if I could get this win, maybe the UFC would come calling. A crazy goal. The best ones often are.

Roddy was fighting that night too and that spurred me on as well. Two lads from council estates on opposite sides of the city. Roddy's fight was the main event and there was no way I was going to allow myself to lose and force him to walk out to a subdued crowd. I wanted him to walk out on a high. John called me and it was time to go. Conor was standing there, and I walked over and gave him a fist bump.

'I'm going to get this fucker for you.'

Sitenkov stood across from me in the cage, expressionless, almost yawning. What the fuck was going on with this guy? Just before the fight was about to start, I heard John say to Ais, 'Do you know what's going to happen here?'

'No,' Ais responded.

'Neither do I,' said John. I didn't want to turn around to acknowledge what I had heard. Ais and John's relationship had always been a strange one, so I was unsure of whether to read something into it or not. Regardless, it was not something I wanted to hear seconds before fighting someone so dangerous.

As soon as the fight started, I had one thought: don't let him overhook. I tried to inch closer and closer, to land a jab, but before I knew it he rushed me against the fence, and took an overhook. Sitenkov wrapped up my leg, but I immediately thought of the little technique I had been working on, blocked the leg and dropped him. Somehow I found myself on top but it was a momentary victory, because he rolled me away, forced my leg out straight and we began rolling. He had my leg extended, cleared the foot off and rolled through, but I caught his arm, something I learned from the sleepless nights of watching that video. But then we rolled again, this time leaving me inverted and upside down with my leg bent like a banana going over my head.

'It's going to break, it's going to break,' I was thinking, fearing the worst. I turned my hip and all of a sudden that was it, a loud clicking sound. My leg came free and I suspected it was broken but when I looked down, somehow, it was okay. We ended up rolling again until eventually I ended up in guard with an overhook.

'If I get this guy now, I have him,' I told myself. Sitenkov felt different all of a sudden. His body was like an empty vessel, his soul no longer on board. He didn't have the fight in him and it was my turn to submit the submission artist. He took the overhook, I reached back, stepped over, and grabbed him in a triangle. I looked over at John.

'Yes, yes!' he screamed at me. I locked in the triangle and that was it, the politest tap I had ever experienced. Even in submission and facing a blackout, Sitenkov remained composed. I rolled off the trigger, stood up, and looked down at my hands.

'I did it. I fucking did it.'

The place erupted into whistles, cheers and beers, everyone was screaming my name. I jumped up on the side of the cage and held my finger up in the air.

'I'm number one in this country now. I'm the fucking best.'

I jumped back down, walked to the middle and sat down next to Sitenkov. We couldn't speak the same language, but the mutual respect was there for all to see. When I got out of the cage, I walked past Neil Seery and Paul Redmond in the front row and both shook my hand.

'Nice one for getting him,' Paul said.

But there was no time to waste. Roddy was getting ready to make his walk so I didn't even go back to the changing room. I stood cageside, with my wraps and shorts still on.

'C'mon Roddy! Let's do it! The two of us are walking out of here together as fucking legends of the game!'

The arena was hopping now, the crowd jumping up and down, and there was no way Roddy was ever going to let them down.

He got the decision against Shannon Gugerty, and after I'd conquered the Bond villain, it was another great night for SBG.

Paddy Holohan, 9-0 — July 2012

Beating Sitenkov meant that I was crowned the Grand Prix Bantamweight Champion before my final fight against Paul McVeigh. There was only one negative.

'There's no belt,' I was told. 'You have to get it back off Paul.'

It was so frustrating. I had to chase people for my money after the fight too. I found myself running around Dublin to different gyms to pick up instalments from people who owed John Ferguson, the promoter, money. I had to go to Lucan to collect a couple of hundred, then off to another gym to collect another hundred and then I was getting vouchers for the Fightstore instead of cash. It was a real kick in the bollocks. I had put everything into my preparation and execution, but my experience was soured by the financial side of things and it made me feel worthless. I had beaten someone who not a lot of people would dare share a cage with, yet found myself with no money and no belt.

To make things worse, no one fought my corner either. We just didn't have proper structures in place for these things. There was no proper management. The bigger cause was that Irish MMA was growing and that was our goal, but I needed the money. I had a kid at home, I needed to take time off work from the chipper to fight, and I had my own bills to pay. Sunday was always my day with Tiernan and I loved spending time with him after a fight, treating him, but when I woke up the next morning after beating Sitenkov, I didn't have the money. That hurt me more than any punch to the face.

Even though I had won the title, I was still due to fight Paul McVeigh, but he quickly put that to bed with a text to John.

'Listen, I've no interest in fighting Paddy,' he told us. 'He's too young, too good, and I'm too old for this. I actually have a few fights planned already. John Ferguson owes one of my fighters a few quid and never gave it to him, so we're selling that belt too.'

I thought that was hilarious even though I wanted the Cage Contender Bantamweight title so much, but I wasn't surprised.

When the McVeigh fight fell through, John asked me to fight a guy named Paddy Doherty in Belfast on short notice as a favour to him. I was physically and mentally drained. I had fought nine times in two years, including three times in ten months, and they were all tough fights. I needed a break. There was no way I could fight Doherty seven days after coming through a tough battle with Sitenkov. John knew I agreed to most things he asked of me, but this turnaround was just too soon. To make matters worse, he wasn't even going to be there.

'He's shit, Paddy,' he assured me. 'You're going to slaughter him. Just go in there, do this, do that and it'll be over.'

I couldn't do it. 'John, my knee is not in it,' I told him. 'It's just not there. I'm not in the right frame of mind mentally either.'

'Okay then, just leave it,' he said, obviously unhappy.

The doctors ended up making my decision for me. My leg was in a bad way after the knee bar from Sitenkov and kept buckling every time I tried to step on it. When the news came through that I couldn't fight, it was like a trap door opened and the anxiety fell out of my body. I had cleared the entire horizon of bantamweight fighters in the country and there was no one to challenge me. King of the castle, I sucked it in and enjoyed the moment. Still ginger, still skinny, and still the last fucking man standing.

Knee injuries are never good, but the timing of this one allowed me to decompress fully from the madness of the previous twenty-four months. I kept training, and I also began to corner some of the team's fights, including one for Ais in Kansas. She fought for the all-female promotion Invicta and although I was ecstatic to be a part of such a big opportunity for her, operating as Ais's cornerman often put me in a difficult position. John was my coach and Ais was my friend and training partner. Sometimes they were on good terms, other times they were not. I stayed out of it as much as I could because I was on my own path, but Ais was my friend and I felt I could offer value in her corner.

My personal life was okay at the time too; okay in the sense that Denise and I weren't at each other's throats every waking minute of the day, so we decided to get a house together. While I was in Kansas cornering Ais, Denise found a house in Raheen for us, not too far from my mam. It was an exciting time in my life, coming home to a new house with my small family. Unfortunately, every week, there seemed to be a new headache with the house.

I was asleep one morning and could hear the rustle of keys at the door. The door was always causing us hassle, and when we were leaving, we would lock the door from the outside and throw the keys back through the letterbox. Denise had gone on the school run and my first thought was that it was her coming back in. The front door eventually opened but I couldn't hear anyone coming up the stairs. I stayed in bed, trying to hear a noise that would tell me whether it actually was Denise or not, staring at the bedroom door, waiting for her to come in. All of a sudden, a little head with beady eyes popped around my door. A drug addict, but a nimble one at that. He leaned into my room, spotted me in the bed and leaned back out in one controlled movement. He didn't jump, didn't panic, but neither did I.

'The little motherfucker,' I thought to myself. I slipped out of bed and crept over to the door. I looked around the door and there he was, at the top of the stairs, trying to listen for any movement to see if I was still asleep. I caught him with an absolute cannon of shot in the back of the ear, and off he went, tumbling down the stairs faster than you can say Hooligan. To make matters worse, the guy had locked himself into the house.

'We're at war now, mate,' I shouted as I turned around and ran back into my bedroom, my pale arse cheeks shining in the Dublin sunrise. He must have thought I was trying to hide, but he was sorely mistaken as I picked up a baseball bat and a pair of underwear. I stuck on my jocks and got ready for round two. The intruder could see me running down the stairs behind him, scrambling at the lock on the door to try to get it open. I was halfway down the stairs, readying my best baseball swing, when he whipped open the door and slammed it shut again behind him. A temporary reprieve, I thought, as I chased him out into the garden. To my disbelief, he was just casually strolling out the front gate as if nothing had happened.

'Here, mate, if you climb into my gaff like that again, I'll kill you stone dead.'

'I didn't do a thing, mister,' he protested, shrugging his shoulders despite the fact that he had just been caught breaking into a naked man's house and thrown down the stairs. 'I didn't do anything.'

His denial set off a trigger of rage and I couldn't control myself. I thought about Denise and Tiernan, and how dangerously different things could have been had they been in the house on their own. I introduced him to the hurling swing I had learned at street leagues.

'Stop, stop. You're being a scumbag,' one of my neighbours shouted. I turned around, foaming at the mouth, standing there in my Dunnes Stores jocks.

'He could have been in your fucking house!'

'Well, okay, okay,' the neighbour said, retreating back to their own house. Eventually, the intruder jumped over the front wall and off down the road, once again casually strolling at a snail's pace. When the guards eventually turned up at the door, they were of no use.

'I heard you had a break-in?' one of them asked.

'Yeah, but I dealt with it,' I told them. 'I'll show you how he got in and bring you through what happened.'

'No, we're not interested in that. Can we come in for a second?'

I was expecting to make a statement about the break-in, or at least that they were coming to tell me that they had caught the rodent who had snuck into my house, but that wasn't the case.

'Where's the baseball bat?' they wanted to know. 'We heard you assaulted a man in the garden with a baseball bat. You have to deal with these things in a certain way and call the guards.'

'When was I going to do that? When I was stabbed to death lying on the landing in my house?'

I kicked the useless pricks out and told them there was no baseball bat, sticking to the rules of life I had learned up North as a kid and never forgotten. See nothing, say nothing.

CHAPTER 9 ....

The news that John was planning to shut down the gym on the Long Mile Road came out of nowhere. The business was not growing, and he had become disillusioned with the constant financial battle and stress that came with that and, unbeknownst to us, decided to throw in the towel. Some of the team already had their next fights booked, but word trickled through that John was heading over to Iceland to Halli and Gunnar Nelson. Halli had hooked him up with a job in Mjolnir MMA and SBG on the Long Mile Road was going to be no more. Ann, John's sister, took over and began the process of winding up the lease and other existing partnerships with suppliers, but none of us was aware of what was truly going on. There was a lot of uncertainty, particularly when Ann couldn't share a definitive date for when the gym doors would actually shut. Two months passed, and we continued to turn up to teach classes and train for our fights, but the longer it persisted, the more questions were asked.

I couldn't believe John had made such a massive decision without speaking to us. We had all been through a lot together and who knows what direction the rest of us would have gone in had John stayed out in Iceland. He never really shared his emotions; that's just the way he's built. I don't think he told many outside his family about his decision. On a personal level,

I understood John's reasons for moving. Maybe he needed the move to help him deal with everything that was going on. Maybe he was exhausted and needed a break to evaluate the next stage of his life. As fate would have it, the move to Iceland didn't suit. There was a combination of factors, including homesickness, and John decided that he was coming home.

It was a strange feeling. I was delighted my coach and father figure was back again but I was still hurt by the fact that he had moved to Iceland without even a goodbye. That moment was a little black mark in my head, and some of my teammates' heads too, because it questioned the true commitment of John to our careers. We were teaching classes for free and it just would have been nice to have gotten a heads-up before John split. The people rowing the boat were left to fend for themselves because the captain fled when the seas became choppy. When John came back, there was no explanation given, no apologies shared, and we all just got on with it. We put the oars back in the water and just kept on rowing to the next fight.

It was around that time my thoughts started shifting to the next stage of my career. One night, I found myself sitting in my mate's house, drinking and smoking while watching the UFC. I was always obsessed with all aspects of the sport, and even watching was an opportunity for me to learn something while unwinding. It must have been a poor card because I fell asleep, only to wake up to the sight of the UFC President Dana White announcing that there was now going to be a series of The Ultimate Fighter at my weight, 135lb. I was in a trance, completely transfixed by this opportunity.

'I'm going to be on that,' I told the lads. 'I'm going to be on that Ultimate Fighter, boys.' It was the first time the UFC had introduced the lower-weight classes and that gave me more confidence.

Their reaction was mixed; one or two believed me, but the other two were half asleep because we were about thirty cans deep and the room was hotboxed liked a sauna. From that moment on, the plan to get Paddy to Las Vegas and The Ultimate Fighter auditions was set in motion. I was sitting in my mate's house in Jobstown, but I knew I would get my day in the UFC.

Time was tight, and money was even tighter. Regardless, I just knew that if I got to Las Vegas, I would make it on to the show. I contacted Rob Connolly in Dublin Ink, a sponsor of mine.

'Rob, I'm trying to get to The Ultimate Fighter. I don't have any money but I know if I can get there, I can do something really special.' Without stuttering, Rob transferred €1,300 over to me immediately, displaying the measure of the man. The night Conor made his UFC debut, we all gathered in John's apartment while the lads took care of business in Sweden. Ais had keys and we watched Conor KO Marcus Brimage with ease. It was incredible to see Conor deliver on that stage, and it drove me to succeed even further.

Departure day rolled around and I found myself in the airport getting ready to leave. I would have loved John to travel with me, but it just wasn't possible. It was an opportunity for me to realise my dream, conquer new ground and, alone or not, I was going to do everything I could to get on to that show. While I was waiting for my flight, my phone rang, and it was John with an offer.

'I have a contract for you with Cage Warriors,' he said. 'It's for a four-man tournament. Sign the contract and send it back to me.' The four-man tournament included Mikael Silander and Dustin Ortiz and I was going to fight both of them on the same night for a total of £1,750.

'I can't sign that, John,' I told him. 'I can't sign a contract like that. I'm at the departure gate, waiting to fly to Vegas for The Ultimate Fighter.'

'Just sign the contract and send it back to me, Paddy,' he insisted. 'I need it signed right now. It's going to be for a world title. Get it back to me.' And he hung up the phone.

There was no way I could sign that contract. I didn't ring John back, and I didn't sign the contract either, a decision that would prove vital just two days later when I was sitting in the Palace Station Hotel waiting for The Ultimate Fighter trials to begin. A representative of the UFC walked into the room.

'Anybody that's under contract, I want you to put your hands in the air,' he announced. There was movement from some of the cockier fighters, launching their hands in the air with pride.

'Okay, get the hell out,' he told them. 'Y'all have to leave.' Bullet dodged. I took my own advice, went with my gut, and saved myself. It was a huge moment for me because it was the first time I realised that standing up for myself was the right thing to do.

At that time, none of us had a penny so we all had individual agreements with John. Coaches would usually get 10% of a fighter's purse, but he had shaken my hand and said, 'You teach classes in my gym for free, keep doing what you're doing, and get as much money in as you can.' It was an honourable move and I shook his hand, looking him straight in the eye. I must have taught three classes per week for four years, and I didn't earn a penny from it. Not that I minded at the time, however;

I was purely focused on the task at hand. I viewed coaching as an apprenticeship and it gave me great energy to help others.

There were no guarantees when I landed in Vegas and headed to the trials at Palace Station. I just had to make an impression. It was scary because I was flat broke with no idea how I was going to repay the loans I had taken to get to America. Adam Nolan, my good friend, came with me, and we somehow went from a sofa in Dublin to a hotel in Vegas in a matter of weeks. We booked a room at Circus Hotel down the end of the strip and couldn't believe it was so cheap.

'This place has a rollercoaster in it. It can't be that bad.'

I had plans of going up and down the rollercoaster before the trials, trying to get the adrenalin pumping, but soon changed my mind. On our first night in Vegas, Adam decided to order a pizza and go to sleep. When we woke, the pizza was making a beeline for the door with thousands of ants marching it out of the room. The place was more council flat than Las Vegas hotel. There was no way I was risking the rollercoaster after that.

When we arrived to the trials, there were fighters of every shape, size and design. The limit was 135lb, but some of the people weighed closer to 185lb. There were guys dressed in full gladiator outfits on, all trying to stand out.

'What the fuck are you looking at?' I snapped back at anyone who caught eyes with me. Two guys who stood out were Davey Grant and Michael Wooten, English fighters who trained with SBG Manchester. Davey was dressed up as Geri Halliwell from the Spice Girls, Union Jack dress and all.

'I'm getting on this. I have kids at home, I need this,' he told me. I admired his determination, but a miniskirt was probably a step too far for me. They packed all 380 of us into a function room in the hotel, with Dana White and Clay Guida walking by every so often. I was nervous, but Adam was really panicking.

'Oh my God, Paddy! Can I go over and get a picture?'

'Act cool man, sit down. They're supposed to want us, not the other way around!'

They could only select sixteen male and sixteen female athletes, so the competition was fierce. I was thinking to myself, 'If I get picked for this stage, I've already made it.'

Eighteen hours passed and we were still in the room. I was drinking coffee, jumping up and down in my chair every so often, doing all I could to stay alert and awake. The first part of the day involved being split into groups, before being called into a little room to roll in front of the judges. The next section involved more groups, except this time we were hitting pads. Thirty seconds was all each of us had, a tiny opportunity to make a splash. I came up against a small American who tried to double-leg me, but I guillotined him straight away. Easy. In the previous season, Dana gave guys $100 for each submission, so I decided I'd try to catch his attention.

'What's the story with my hundred dollars, Dana?' I needed that money, but he just laughed. I passed the rolling stage. Next, I passed the pads stage and more people were cut. Finally, it came to the last stage, and it was the one I was most confident about; the interview. Dana White and the producer of The Ultimate Fighter were all that stood between myself and a spot on the show. Some people felt that we all just got UFC contracts off the back of Conor and John's success, and that used to frustrate me. No doubt it helped some fighters, but in my case it wasn't true. My first meeting with the UFC came through my own actions;

my application, my loan, my performance. As we entered the room, I was confident because I knew how charismatic I could be. I sat down, met everyone and Dana asked, 'What are you going to bring to the table?' This was my time to shine and I began to introduce the world to Paddy Holohan.

'Sit back lads, take a minute,' I said, and I began to recite a Tommy Tiernan piece.

'We don't come in here and invade you. We don't turn up with guns and tanks and stuff. We turn up in an infestation. That's what we do. I'll turn up, and there's going to be me, my mate Conor who just won last week, we'll have a phone number and a sleeping bag, and you won't even notice us. But in ten years' time, ten of us are going to walk out here.'

Dana turned to the producer. 'Oh my God, this kid Conor McGregor was so charismatic. Knocked out Marcus Brimage. So, are you on the same team?'

'Yeah, we all came up together. There's loads of us, Dana, so you better get that chequebook out.' I could see that he was loving the moment, bouncing off everything I said.

'So, what do you love the most?' Dana asked.

'Ireland,' I said. 'It's in my blood.'

The interview finished and I returned to the meeting room, waiting to hear how I had gotten on, all the while becoming more and more anxious. I had been in all types of situations in my life, but this nervousness was different. I needed a spot on that show more than anyone. Sixteen blokes out of 380 people. It was simple; I was either getting on a plane home or heading to the UFC. The guy came out and began to call names. One after the other. No Holohan. Still no Holohan. And then, just as I had given up hope, it happened and they called my name. I couldn't believe it, my chance had finally arrived. The Hooligan was heading to The Ultimate Fighter.

I wasn't allowed to tell anyone that I had made it through, but that didn't stop me getting the message back home. Everyone else left and twenty of us were brought to a room where they gave us further information.

'We're going to give you $100 per day,' we were told. I remember looking at Adam and shouting, 'This is my mate, make sure you don't forget him too!' And they didn't. We both ended up in a lovely room in Palace Station with a swimming pool and all, bidding farewell to the bucket of shite known as Circus Circus. The uncertainty with The Ultimate Fighter is that you're in, but you don't know for how long. I could also see that they had selected twenty people instead of sixteen, so something else was in store. They asked us to fill out a hefty application booklet with all our details but it took forever, so I just decided I'd chance my arm.

'Mate, I can't read or write,' I said. 'I speak Gaelic.'

'Oh, our sincere apologies, Mr Holohan,' the producer said, and took my paperwork to fill it out for me. For some of the American fighters it wasn't so simple; they even failed this part. They were panicking trying to give correct addresses, while I sat with my feet up, thanks to our native language.

I was elated, but there were another few hurdles to jump before I could really relax, one of which was the medical, and that terrified me. I wasn't worried about drugs, because I was a clean athlete save for a few sporadic joints every now and then, but I was certain they would find out about my blood disorder.

'Right, you're all going to be drug-tested now,' they told us. 'When you go home, you will have two months to clear your system for when you return.'

When the time came for my medical, I was shaking with fear. The doctor surely thought that I was trying to hide steroids or worried about failing a drug test, but the two things that worried me were my blood disorder and the brain surgery I had had as a child. I knew the latter would show up on my MRI and had to make a quick decision, so I decided to tell the doctor about my surgery, but not the blood disorder.

'I had blood clots removed from my brain as a young fella and I have a scar on my side,' I explained. I remember even trying to hide the scar throughout the trials, as it constantly played on my mind.

'Don't worry, I'll check this out,' the doctor said as I sat there, looking out the window, wondering if my UFC dream was about to be crushed. Twenty athletes were picked, and only sixteen would progress, so I knew I was in trouble. The doctor returned.

'You have nothing to worry about, I looked at your MRI and it's all good.'

I jumped up from the chair. 'Yes! Fucking delighted I am!'

'Do you have anything else to declare?' he asked.

'Nope, I'm all good, doc,' I said, and I walked out the door.

I arrived back to Dublin a few days later but we were warned by the UFC that if they heard one whisper about the fact that we'd got through, our paperwork would be ripped up and we would be thrown off the show. 'How did you get on?' people kept asking. 'I don't know yet,' I just kept replying, because, to be honest, I didn't. The official confirmation still hadn't come through yet.

A week later, I was sitting in the house in Raheen. I was freezing cold, flat broke, and had spent the morning chopping up old doors to burn them for heat. Even buying a bag of coal was a struggle; I would have to get it one week, and pay for it the next. As I stared into the embers of a burning door I had taken from a skip down the road, I heard the beep of an email landing in my inbox. I leapt up and opened it immediately.

'Congratulations, you have been selected for The Ultimate Fighter. You will receive $1,500 per week for being on the show. You will get "x" for a knockout, "y" for a submission.' I just kept reading and reading, spending every cent in my head. It was time to fly out to Vegas again, but this time I was flying on the UFC's dollar. Flights, accommodation, visa, all sorted, thanks to Dana White and the Ultimate Fighting Championship.

When the day came to head back to America, it was one of the most difficult goodbyes I can remember. Travelling into the unknown was difficult, but saying goodbye to Tiernan was excruciating. I didn't know how long I would be away, but worryingly, I knew I wouldn't be able to take the fibrogammin that I needed to treat my blood condition. The UFC searched everyone's bags and I couldn't risk them learning my big secret. I always understood I was putting my life at risk stepping into the cage, but without my medication, the risk of cranium bleeds increased massively.

Worried as I was, I simply had to take my opportunity in The Ultimate Fighter, if not for me, then for my son. Everything I had worked towards was to create a better life for him, and now that I was so close, I couldn't afford to let it slip away. I took a deep breath, wiped away a tear, and set off for Las Vegas, not knowing if I would ever return.

It was late at night when I arrived into the Palace Station in Las Vegas. I was asked if I needed anything, and foolishly, I declined. Little did I know it then, but I should have grabbed absolutely everything as that hotel room would become my prison for the next four days. I wasn't allowed to leave the room, let alone the hotel, and even my food had to be ordered up directly. Everything was monitored. I had been struggling with a back injury since the fight against Sitenkov. In the weeks afterwards, I could feel this weird sensation but I had forced it to the back of my mind and kept on training, hoping that it would heal itself naturally. Now it was getting worse, and I couldn't even leave the hotel for a foam roller or to train. Being locked away like this was torture, but I made the most of the situation. I put the beds up against the wall and created my own room workout, old-school style. If I was caught outside my room, I would have been sent home immediately and I couldn't take that risk. I just sat there looking out on Las Vegas, taking stock of how far I had come and waiting for the day I would be given the opportunity to fulfil my dream.

Finally, on the fourth day, we were allowed to leave and headed to The Ultimate Fighter gym to find out who our opponents would be. The gym was a sight to behold. There were two big murals of Ronda Rousey and Cat Zingano on the walls, and there was a special aura about the place. It was surreal. I felt like I had been zapped into the telly like Mike Teavee from *Charlie and the Chocolate Factory*. The weigh-in was torturous, though. We sat around all day, starving. Fighters needed to hit 135lb, which wasn't going to be an issue for me, so I ate about fifteen energy bars as that was the only food available. When the fights were announced, I got a tough draw against a wrestler called Josh Hill. Hill was 9-0 and probably the most awkward opponent there. Phones, laptops, iPads were all banned, but that didn't stop me hiding one in my hotel room under my mirror. I sent John a message, telling him I had been drawn against Hill and asking him for tips and advice. John provided a strong game plan: be careful of the take down, he's going to level change, stay low. People might find it strange that I was willing to take the risk of smuggling an iPad into The Ultimate Fighter, but not my medication. For me, it was simple. If they found the iPad, my career would continue, but if they found the medication, it was game over, and that was a risk I was not willing to take.

The day of the fight rolled around and despite my excitement, I just couldn't shake the grogginess. Something that Dana had said at the weigh-in struck a chord with me. 'Make sure you leave it all in there, because you don't want to be heading home on the bus,' and I tried to push that to the front of my mind. I knew Josh Hill was going to be tough, but I didn't consider him dangerous. My back was tingling, but I didn't give a fuck. I was ready for war.

John sent me a song, 'Ten Thousand Hours' by Macklemore and Ryan Lewis. 'I don't really listen to this type of music but when I heard this, I thought of you,' he wrote. 'Good luck today.' Before I left for the fight, I wrote one of the lyrics — '10,000 hands will carry me' — on the mirror and I bade farewell to the iPad. In my mind, I would never be heading back to that hotel room again.

When I arrived at the gym, Josh Hill's family were all there to support him. I missed Tiernan more than ever. I had spent four mentally challenging days in my hotel room, and now I was alone again, fighting to secure my family's future. I wanted the victory more than anything, but strangely, I wanted Hill to beat me up too. It was my twisted way of dealing with my emotions. I was standing at the dressing room door, rubbing my knuckles against my face, ready to make the walk, when every light in the building went out.

'What the fuck?!'

The power had gone in the gym, and we all had to head back to the dressing room while they tried to fix it. An hour later, I made the walk again, but by then my lethargy and general sadness had ballooned and I just wanted to get the fight over with.

When we finally touched gloves I kept hitting Hill with shots, mashing him with elbows on every takedown attempt, but he just wouldn't move. I don't think he even hit me, and he spent the entire fight trying to take me down. I felt my takedown defence was strong at the time, but in truth, it was technically poor. There were times I nearly had him, but my left leg was just dead throughout. I wondered if fatigue was affecting me, and thought I deserved a third round, but the fight didn't go my way. I could hear his family throughout, screaming, 'Get him, Josh. Kill him, Josh!' and all I could think was, 'Fuck you, you're all next.' In the madness of the fight, I thought to myself, 'God, I feel so lonely.' It was horrible. I lost on a decision and felt terrible. I walked straight over to Dana White and Ronda Rousey, who was one of the team coaches.

'Dana, make me a promise,' I said. 'When you come back to Dublin, give me a 125lb fight. I'm not a 135-pounder. You saw that sack of shite in there hanging out of me and he was struggling.' To be fair to Dana, when the episode aired on television, he said, 'Josh Hill will never fight in the UFC. What a boring fight.' It didn't matter. I was heading home.

I felt fucking awful and was disgusted with myself. Paddy Holohan's first loss, the fucking failure. I had gone over there to create a better life for my family, better than the one I had grown up with, and now here I was, coming back as a complete and utter failure. It meant everything to me. As fate would have it, I would eventually turn out to be one of the most successful applicants on The Ultimate Fighter that season, but I didn't know it then, and it stung. Sometimes the lesson is not in the moment, and the moment becomes the lesson, but it took me a long time to figure that out.

Paddy Holohan, 9-0 (One Unofficial Exhibition Loss) — May 2013

Losing at The Ultimate Fighter crushed me. When I came home, people constantly asked me about the experience, and it was made all the worse by the fact that I wasn't allowed to say anything. The first night after losing, I headed to the pub alone for some liquid therapy. I had a pint of Guinness in front of me, and one lad just kept talking. On and on, and on and on, to the point where I just couldn't take it any more. I remember saying to myself, 'I am going to kill him. I feel like cracking my fist off his skull.' I left the pint there and headed back to my room. I had so many different emotions, and the only way I had been programmed to deal with them was through violence, a risky way to live life.

I was straight up with everyone that was close to me. I told them that I was a failure, my dream was over and that I didn't make it to the UFC. I remember saying to Denise, 'That's it. I can't go back. I'm done. I simply cannot go back to the grind of fighting in small arenas for €500. My dream has gone.' The depression worsened and I began to seriously contemplate walking away from it all. Mixed martial arts had given me such amazing highs, but this latest low was becoming impossible. As much as I tried, I couldn't shift the black cloud. What made things worse was that nobody really noticed how down I was. During difficult times in life, it can become a slippery slope. It's very easy to fall into a dark place and not know if you're going to come out. My life felt like it was over. I was devastated and felt lower than ever. I could not see a way out and considered freeing myself of all the pain and anguish. Fuck learning, my life was over and nobody seemed to give a shit.

On top of that, my back injury was getting worse and worse to the point where it began affecting my daily life. On the flight home to Ireland, I had to lie down on the floor of the plane as I couldn't sit down on the nerve. When I got back home, I found myself sleeping on the landing, just like I had all those years ago when I was kicked out of my bedroom. It's funny how life works; I had devoted years of my life to fulfilling my dreams, but here I was right back where I started. It got to the point where I couldn't even lie down, I had to stand vertically and lean against the landing window. I spent a couple of weeks standing in that position. Awake or asleep, I just had to stand.

I was losing weight, couldn't eat properly, and hadn't gone back to the gym in a while. Denise and I weren't intimate, and our relationship had deteriorated to the point where it was non-existent. Months were passing without physical contact. It was as if her mind was somewhere else. And in a way, I can understand some of it. I was losing my masculinity and had become a shadow of myself. I read text messages on Denise's phone from a guy. He was a work-husband, if you must, that guy who was always too forward with her. One day I was out in the leisure centre swimming with Tiernan, and he introduced himself with a handshake that didn't feel too friendly. I knew by looking at him, that there was more to this guy and that I would have to watch him around Denise. Excuses came through — 'Ah, he's only a friend.' There were times she was supposed to stay in her friend's house in Bray, but I would offer to collect her and she would panic and come straight home. I wasn't stupid. I knew something was going on. I wasn't upset, not to the point where I was heartbroken and wanted to break down, but I was curious. I wanted to know what was going on.

I was experiencing so many different and dark emotions. I could barely look my son in the eyes without feeling like I had failed him. My self-esteem had hit rock bottom and I was back to being the skinny, angry, dark kid of my youth. I was depressed, even if I couldn't admit it — but what benefit would acknowledging my depression's existence give me? I still felt like shit, and being around Denise just seemed to exacerbate the situation. The arguments worsened and the distance between us grew. I was losing my childhood sweetheart, the mother of my son, and I felt nothing but apathy. I had no motivation to do anything. She was doing her own thing, and I was a broken man.

One or two from the gym reached out to me, but I don't think anyone really knew how badly I was feeling. When it came to helping me deal with my back injury, John Connor, a coach from the Irish Strength Institute, did more for me than I could have asked for. He gave me free stretches, dry needling, and did all he could to help. I physically reached rock bottom when walking Tiernan to his friend's house one morning. My back locked up, and I fell straight to the floor, unable to move. Tiernan was so upset, looking at me lying in the grass, unable to help his father, tears flowing down both of our faces.

'Are you okay, Dad?'

'Just go and get your ma, Tiernan.'

I must have been there for fifteen minutes, lying in the field, motionless, crying. And of course, it started to piss rain too. A pathetic fallacy for a pathetic man. Why me? Why did I go through such a shitty childhood for it all to just end like this? It wasn't supposed to end like this for me. I had visions of coming home after winning The Ultimate Fighter and handing money to my coach, my son, to the people who mattered, but here I was, soaking wet from a mix of tears and rain, lying helpless in a field in Dublin.

The Hooligan inside me awoke again. 'Don't fucking quit. Not now. Get up! Get up!' That voice was the only person that was there for me in the darkest of times. It gave me the push I needed. I'd love to say that I improved instantly, but that wasn't the case. I still had moments of misery, but at least I now had a microscopic drop of motivation in my body, a place that had felt no hope or happiness for too long.

My mindset improved but my back injury worsened. Training was a no-go. I could barely walk, and it was a struggle to tie my laces. I wasn't into painkillers because I had seen the destruction prescription drugs could bring to a home, and wasn't going to risk it for Tiernan. I decided enough was enough, and it was time to go see a specialist.

This particular surgeon was unlike any of the others I had met, though. Keith Synnott was his name, a small man with a dickie bow. He had a track record and had performed surgery on Paul O'Connell, the Irish rugby captain. The minute we caught eyes, I knew he was different. I felt comfortable in his presence immediately. He told me that I had a herniated disc, confirming my worries.

'I need surgery badly,' I told him. 'You need to cut me open and fix my back. I have to make it back to the UFC or else I'm going to end up killing myself. I genuinely need this.' I had become obsessed with back pain and injuries, consuming every piece of information on the internet in search of an answer. As well as that, there were rumours that the UFC was returning to Ireland the following year, so I knew I was under pressure to be fit if they did come knocking.

'Okay, that's no problem,' he said. 'I'll do the surgery, let's get you a date.' I couldn't believe it. He was going to fix me.

People wrote me off and said my career was over, but history should have taught them that the Hooligan never gives up. The surgery was a success, and it was as if the pain had been let out of me like a balloon being deflated. I felt fucking great, and I had plenty of time to get ready for the potential UFC card in January. I went hell for leather into rehab for eight weeks working with John Connor. We started with stomach flexes before advancing to walking up and down stairs, and I could feel myself getting back to full fitness. I had a clear goal and I was achieving it. My mind was in a better place and just nine short weeks later, I was back in the gym performing front and back tumbles. A life of living with Velcro shoes didn't look as likely any more. I felt like I was reborn.

Anyone that has dealt with back pain knows just how dark life can become. I refused to take pain medication throughout my rehab as I was fully aware of the damage and destruction it can bring to a home.

I was feeling really good and rolling with Ais in the gym one day when all of a sudden: pop. My back gave way again. The pain I had felt the first time around was nothing compared to excruciating sensation I experienced that day. It felt like cold water running down through the nerve in my lower back and my leg, but this time it was on the opposite side and I was motionless. I wanted to cry, and the darkness returned immediately. This was my worst fear, and I didn't feel confident about being able to overcome my demons a second time. I went straight to the hospital and begged them to do something for the pain. They gave me an injection in my back but it was no use. My toes were numb and I had cold feet. The hospital contacted Mr Synnott and sent me home while I waited to meet him later that week. I was fully convinced that this was the end, and that I was destined to just finish my career in my early twenties. I even contemplated kidnapping the surgeon, dragging him back to my house and making him perform the surgery in my freezing cold Raheen kitchen. I was that desperate. When I met him, he reassured me.

'Let me tell you something, son, do not be worried. I'll do the surgery again. This is normal. Sometimes it's like a grape, you squeeze it and a little bit squirts out and then you cut it off. Then it takes a little while for the last little bit to come out and you cut that off then and it's grand. Don't worry.'

I couldn't believe it, another chance.

Because of my medical history, there was a lot of communication between Mr Synnott and the haemophilia staff and it ended up going on my file. I didn't have time to worry about that. The surgery was set for 13 December 2013, which would give me a chance to fight on the UFC card when they finally confirmed a Dublin card. I prayed Dana White was a man of his word. By this time, the advertisement for The Ultimate Fighter had started to air and I was on the front of it. People were going crazy — 'Oh my God, Paddy. I knew you'd do it' — but it was horrible. I knew I was a failure.

The second surgery was a success and I felt even smoother this time. I horsed through rehab and was laser-focused on getting back to my best, but halfway through, the scar on my back got infected and filled up with pus. I went straight into hospital to get rid of it but there was immediate panic. They didn't know if it was pus or whether synovial fluid was leaking into my spinal cord as a result of the surgery. It turned out that it was infected fluid and they removed it before treating me with a course of antibiotics in the hospital for a few days. I had a reaction to the antibiotics, however, and my arm started to swell and my chest broke out in massive boils. I went into convulsions. They ripped the IV out of my hand, but my body had gone into shock. It turned out I was allergic to the antibiotic they were using, the only thing I'd ever been allergic to in my life. Hives formed all over my body while the doctors stabilised me. I spent the next couple of weeks confined to a hospital bed while word came through that the UFC was coming to Dublin in July. That gave me about five months to beat the infection if Dana White came calling.

'Any day now,' I thought to myself. 'Any day now they're going to call.' But, just to make sure I was there no matter what, I bought two tickets for the event and then won another two in a poker tournament. The tickets were like gold dust and UFC Dublin sold out immediately.

Five weeks out from the show, there was still no call. I was driving through Dublin, down the canal, and a call came in from a number I didn't recognise.

'How would you like to fight in the UFC?' John asked, calling from the fight camp in Iceland. Boom! I threw the phone on the floor and nearly swerved into the water.

'Yeeeessssss!' I pulled into the side of the road and started to scream again. 'Yes! Yes! Yes!' punching the steering wheel. I gathered myself as best I could and rang John back.

'Are you alright, Paddy?'

'Fuckin' right I'll fight in the UFC.'

I couldn't describe the emotions. I was all over the place, and even drove into the wrong housing estate on my way back to Tallaght. I couldn't think straight, I was consumed by thoughts of the UFC. Paddy Holohan fighting on the main card of UFC Fight Night 46, headlined by none other than my teammate and friend Conor McGregor.

I rang Denise. 'Where are ya? Where are ya?' I sped to the shopping centre, threw open my door and jumped out. 'I've signed for the UFC. I'm fighting in Dublin in five weeks.'

My dream was becoming a reality. I didn't know who I was going to fight, but I didn't care. I would have fought King fucking Kong that night. I was 9-0 in my professional career in Europe and headed to the UFC, a spot I had earned through years of blood, sweat and cauliflower ears. Just months earlier I had been lying

down in a wet field, crying, unable to move. Now here I was, ready
to shake up the world with a UFC fight in my own back yard.

CHAPTER 10 ....

I f I ever thought that my opportunity had passed, that changed once I got that phone call from John. He was in Iceland, which was quickly becoming our go-to place for fight camps, due to our connection with the Mjolnir MMA gym and Halli Nelson, Gunni's dad, who was acting as Conor's manager at the time. Conor was already over there with John as well as Cathal Pendred, James Gallagher, Philip Mulpeter and Kiefer Crosbie.

'You're going to have to make it over to Iceland,' John said.

I was in a rush to get over, but I didn't have a pot to piss in at the time and was flat broke. I didn't even know how much I was going to make for my UFC fight, but just knew it was going to be a lot more than €100 in fight vouchers.

Eventually, after scraping a few pennies together thanks to Rob Connolly at Dublin Ink again, I booked the next flight and found myself in Reykjavik Airport. As I was waiting for my bag, I got a call from a neurologist, Dan Healy, one of the few people who knew about my blood condition. I had decided not to tell him that I had signed for the UFC, but he heard anyway.

'You're going to have to tell the UFC about your blood condition. This is too dangerous. We will deal with whatever happens.'

I cut him off mid-sentence. 'I'm telling you now. Don't you dare say anything. This is doctor-patient confidentiality. Don't you dare say a fucking word.'

'Paddy, you're taking a huge risk,' he reminded me. 'You could die in there. The worst case is that they take you off the card, that's it.'

I cut him off again. 'Dan, listen. I have nothing. My family have nothing. This is my only opportunity. I could have died on that little road in Jobstown and never made it. I just want five or six fights and then I'll bow out. This is my chance to be somebody. Do not stand in my fucking way.' And I hung up the phone.

When I landed in Iceland, Halli, John and John's girlfriend, Orlagh, picked me up and headed to the place where I'd be staying. It was about 1am and we pulled up outside a nice apartment.

'Nice one,' I said and started to gather my stuff.

'No, no, Paddy,' John said. 'You're not staying here, this is for me and Orlagh. You're staying in another spot, Halli is going to bring you there. I'll see you on Monday. Conor is in the other gaff, head down there.'

Halli dropped me off at some random spot. 'It's in there,' he pointed, up towards a set of stairs, and drove off. I walked up the stairs, unsure what was waiting for me at the top. Before I knew it, a pair of recognisable young eyes peered out the window.

'It's fucking Paddaaay,' James Gallagher shouted in his northern Irish brogue. I walked into the house and the place looked like it had been turned upside down. Plates on the table and clothes all over the ground. Conor was upstairs with Dee, his partner, but Kiefer Crosbie and James were there to greet me. James escorted me to my lodgings and it was nothing more than a dog bed in the corner with a dirty sheet. By now, he had been telling me about all of the madness that had taken place, so there was absolutely no chance of me sleeping there. It wasn't that the lads were drinking or anything, it was just them cooking, blaring music, cooking bacon and eggs at 3am and just lads being lads.

'If you think I'm sleeping in that yoke, you have another think coming,' I told him. 'I'd fail a medical after a night in that yoke. Kiefer, I'm bunking with you.' Kiefer was staying in the sitting room in a double bed, with a curtain pulled across for privacy, and that was good enough for me. We ended up sharing a cage during the day, and a bed at night. It was rough living but it was better than sleeping in that crusty dog bed.

We were like superheroes in Iceland. Everyone knew why we were there. Mjolnir MMA was amazing and they looked after us so well. Halli did everything he could for us. The training was solid. John was taking the sessions and I sparred with James and a lot of the Icelandic guys. After a couple of days sparring, I felt invincible inside the cage. Things got even better when one of the local fighters, Sunna Davidsdottir, aka Sunna Tsunami, said she had a spare room that I could move into.

'I feel like you need to rest sometimes if you are to be your best.'

The living situation in the gaff with the lads was fine for a while, but I needed to get my head straight. They were late risers, meaning they stayed up late too, and that didn't suit me. 'No hard feelings, but I just need a bit of peace,' I admitted, and to be fair, they accepted it. I remember Conor saying, 'Paddy, you do whatever you have to do to get to where you need to be. You'll get nothing but respect from us for it.' It was great to hear that, because it was a little bit awkward telling the lads I didn't want to live with them. The room at Sunna's was small, but much more spacious than sharing a bed with Kiefer behind a curtain. It even had a goldfish, and I christened him Robbie Keane after the Irish footballer, a fellow Jobstownian. I found out later that Sunna had named him Mufasi, so I re-christened him Mufasi Keane. I could fully focus on my training and not worry about where to sleep that night, especially considering it was the time of year in Iceland when there was twenty-four hours of light per day. It was beautiful, but tough. I would finish training late at night, put my headphones in and run through the bright streets of Reykjavik all the way to the sea. It was surreal. Bright outside, but not a sinner to be seen. After two weeks of serenity, the room in Sunna's house was needed by someone else so I had to move back in with the lads.

'Lads, I've got to move back into the gaff,' I told them, 'but fuck sharing the bed. I'm staying upstairs with you, Conor.' Conor had the penthouse suite of the apartment, if such a thing existed, and had the privilege of being able to come downstairs for shenanigans but being able to retreat to the peace when he'd had enough. We were training harder than ever so Conor was happy to have the company.

It didn't take a fight or two in the UFC to prove to me that Conor was the real deal. We could see from an early age that he was different. Years before he made his UFC debut, I looked over at Conor and Gunni hitting a bag upstairs in the Long Mile gym after one of Conor's boxing classes and said to my friend Stephen Dunne, 'See them? Gunni is going to go to the UFC first, and then Conor's going to go, and I guarantee you he will blow this entire game out of the water.' At that time, nobody would fight Conor. It was near impossible to get an opponent for him, everyone knew what he was capable of. People were pretending to crash at the airport and missing their flights just to avoid fighting him.

He had incredible movement, an obsession with the craft and the correct mindset. When we were sharing a room in Iceland, I woke up countless times in the middle of the night to the sight of Conor watching videos about boxing and wrestling on his iPad. 'Did you ever see this?' he would shout across to me in my bed, keeping his eyes focused solely on the iPad. I'd answer but he wouldn't even acknowledge it. He never took his eye off the ball.

We spent five weeks in the camp in Iceland, and then it was time to go home to Jobstown for the final preparations. Denise and I had said goodbye to the house in Raheen, but also to our relationship. We both knew things were not the same as before, and the inevitable needed to happen. She was still there for me, always a great mother for Tiernan, and even ended up coming to the UFC Dublin card.

Fight week was a circus: registering, weight cuts, weigh-ins, poster signings and, of course, fight night itself. The UFC gave me a hotel room in Dublin city centre and I remember getting the Luas from Tallaght and checking in. The woman at the UFC desk handed me €500 cash as a per diem payment.

'I live here in Dublin, and you're paying me per diem?' The UFC was definitely a step up. I finished signing posters, and even though my hand was hopping, it still felt pretty cool. I had to pick my walk-out song but the song I wanted to use, 'The Rocky Road to Dublin', had already been taken by another fighter. I ended up going with 'Ten Thousand Hours', the song I had used at The Ultimate Fighter. I took the Luas back to The

Square shopping centre in Tallaght and bought myself three pairs of runners with my per diem cash. It was always about the simple things for me, but I liked to look fresh. The days of the Dunnes Stores boxer shorts were finally in the rear-view mirror.

I was cutting weight all week so I was only allowed to nibble chicken and drink coffee, but I felt great. Years later, Adam told me that it was the happiest and, at the same time, the most nervous he had ever seen me. Skin and bones, but laughing my head off. Word filtered through that I was going to be first on the card. That would have made most people nervous, but I saw it as an opportunity to write my name into history as the first Irishman to get a victory in the UFC on Irish soil. It was all about Ireland for me. Tom Egan had been the first Irishman to attempt to get a victory in the UFC in Ireland back in 2009, and sitting in that arena as a kid, watching a fellow Irishman make that walk, gave me the energy and enthusiasm to become a fighter. Now it was this kid's time to plant that Irish flag in the centre of the octagon.

On the day of the weigh-in, I had to be in the Ibis Hotel at 8am. I cut seven pounds in the hotel bath. The weight cut can be extremely draining and during the week of a fight, I would begin my water-loading by drinking six litres, before gradually dropping it down to five, and then four, and then cutting it out completely. If I was weighing in on a Friday, I cut water on Wednesday night and would drink nothing further until after weigh-in. The diet was always chicken and almond butter, the latter because it helps to activate the proteins and enzymes in the chicken. John had gotten that information from Mickael Daboville's coach, and we stuck to it. Three chicken fillets a day with almond butter spread on it and nothing else, not even a vegetable. By the end of that week, my entire digestive system was in bits. My body reminded me of the M50 motorway; it was either all jammed up, or plenty of flowing traffic. Constipation was always an issue, but dandelion water helped to combat that. Some people were taking caffeine tablets, but I was never one for that. The only caffeine I was getting was from my other obsession: tea. I drank tea throughout all my camps and sometimes I'd even take sugar. People thought I was mad. 'I gave up everything in my life for this, but there's no way I'm stopping with the tea!' Chicken and nut butter for a week, water-loading for five days, and then a few cups of tea in between and that was it.

I was feeling fresh for this particular cut, though, even though it was my first time to drop to flyweight. Never in my life had I made 125lb, but when the UFC asked me to do it, I was doing it. I would have starved myself to the point of near death and made 115lb if they asked me. That was my mindset. Any weight class, any contract. I'll do it. It became an obsession. I weighed myself at least fifty times every day, and it was how I would imagine life with an eating disorder. After every bathroom break, I would weigh myself. The weighing scales can be a hugely addictive thing, and jumping on and off them all day can have a huge bearing on your mental health. When it came to the weigh-in, I think I was 134lb on the day, and needed to cut to 125lb. I was expecting it to be high as I was full of water from water-loading, and had taken no salt, so the sodium in my body was still dropping out.

I spent twenty minutes in the bath that day, fully naked. Adam was looking after me, but John was in the hotel too, running from room to room trying to oversee everyone's weight cut. I would lie in the bath, nice and warm, to make me sweat. It was better than any sauna because it was a heat you could control, rather than an intense heat. There were times I repeated this for up to ten hours; twenty minutes in, twenty minutes out, wrapped up on the floor. We put salt in the bath and even nail varnish remover too, sometimes, to open the pores. I was a psychopath in the bath. I would jump in and start singing 'Rattlin' Bog' to keep my mind off it. Some people were silent when going through the bath and it worked for them, but I was the opposite. I would think about everything when I was in there; life, purpose, family, the future. I found comfort in it.

I didn't know how difficult cutting to 125lb was going to be. I would end up fighting five times in fifteen months, cutting more than 20lb for each fight, and then putting it back on. My body weighed 125lb in total, and over the course of those five fights, I cut a whopping 110lb. There was a lot of miseducation around cutting at the time, and I often wondered about how damaging it truly was. My testicles would get so sore during the cut, it felt like they were in a vice and being tightened with every dip in and out of the water. I was draining my body of fluid, and it affected everything. Infertility was always a worrying thought in the back of my mind. My body would send warning signals and tell me in certain ways that the cut was having a negative effect, but I just had to continue. I was drained of everything except will and spirit, and that determination would see me through almost anything.

This particular cut was a difficult one. Gunni had 4lb or so to cut, and Conor was the same as me, hating the cut but knowing we would get through it. He had to hit 145lb, and Cathal was cutting serious weight too, but he was a pro at it. In my head, when I was struggling in my room, everyone else was going through the same struggles, so I would just force myself to get on with it. I was so drained of everything that I had to be carried out of the bath, sucking ice cubes for moisture as I hadn't drunk water in over a day. As the final part of my cut approached, I still had a pound to go so I just wrapped myself up like a mummy and made sure to keep warm. Gunni was in the same position, but it was just a quick sweat for him. He always walked around at close to fight weight, but he must have had an extra dessert at dinner. The two of us just lay in a hotel room together. We barely said a word, I didn't have the energy to. The funny side of it was that sometimes the hotel staff were clueless to the situation and would call up to the room when we rang down for extra towels and salt. The look on their face was always one of horror when they could see twenty towels on the floor and ten people lowering a naked man into a bath.

When we arrived at the weigh-in, we had to wait backstage before being called. It felt like the longest wait of my career. I was so close to finally getting a drink of water and would have licked sweat off a used jockstrap just to get a bit of moisture. I was parched, dry to my crusty eyeballs. Nearly there, I told myself. The weigh-in at the time was the same as the ceremonial weigh-in, meaning I had to weigh-in in front of thousands of people. If I missed weight, that was it. Here were guys sitting in the front row with burgers and chips and pints in their hands, casting aspersions on us — 'How dare he miss weight?' — stuffing themselves. It was like standing in front of a judge and jury of drunk people who were waiting to send you down.

I looked at the opposite corner of the room and could see my opponent Josh Sampo sitting on the ground in a puddle, drained. I could see he had nothing left and tried to catch his eye as an intimidation tactic, to let him know that I was going to fucking kill him. Telepathically I was trying to break his psyche and tell him there was no chance he was leaving my hometown with anything but a defeat. My mindset was similar to previous fights; if I murdered him and it meant everyone cheered, then I'd be happy to do it.

I was the first person on the card, meaning I was the first Irish person to weigh-in. John Connor made the walk with me and that was important because he had given me so much. I was gaunt and stripped of every ounce of energy in my body, but standing in front of the hometown crowd gave me a boost like a shot of adrenalin. I had the Irish flag with me, the same one I've used throughout the years, each bloodstain a reminder of every beast I had slain, and marched proudly onto the scales. As I stared out at the crowd, I recognised so many faces. These were my people. I could feel every eye on me. It was my moment. I took a deep breath, my arms outstretched, and let out a roar at the top of my lungs, absorbing as much of the crowd's energy as possible. It was life-giving.

We both made weight and readied ourselves for the face-off. I stepped up and could see it in Josh Sampo's eyes, the same look I had seen so many times before. I was staring into his soul and there was nothing there. He was a mere mortal, and I felt like Goliath. This time, there would be no underdog victory.

We walked off stage and I downed a coconut water concoction that John Connor had made and went to get a good view of the rest of the lads weighing in. After he had made weight, Conor grabbed the mic and shouted, 'Tomorrow I take his head clean off!' I was standing with the crowd and the power of those words reverberated throughout Dublin.

On our way back to the hotel, I started to feel discomfort in my stomach. The coconut water. We arrived in the lobby and

I started walking faster and faster, speed-walking through the lobby to get to my room. 'There's Paddy Holohan,' someone who recognised me shouted. I stood by the lift, hammering the call button viciously. Even the press circled me looking for interviews. Finally, the elevator arrived and I jumped in and rushed to my room. It went from my lip to my hip in a matter of seconds and the heavens opened in that bathroom; it was the last time I would ever drink coconut water directly after weighing in. I was even more dehydrated after the explosion in Room 205, so I filled up on water and used an IV drip to get some nutrients and fluids back into me. You need the IV so that your body can break down food after you've weighed in, and it's a huge boost after a torturous week. They were permitted by the UFC at the time and despite people having the perception that the UFC organised IVs for fighters, that wasn't the case. We had to arrange for a guy to come to the hotel and administer drips to all of us.

That night a group of us went to a restaurant in the city for a couple of hours, but instead of getting a taxi back with everyone else, I decided I would do my own thing and stroll back. I walked alongside the River Liffey, staring at the lights of Dublin city. The sky was clear and crisp, and I found myself in a place in my life where I felt happy. I knew the UFC Dublin card was going to be special and talked about for years, but I just hoped I would come out on the right side of history. At that moment, in the build-up to that fight, I knew there was no chance I was going to lose. I would have beaten anyone. I walked past the arena and thought about how far we had come. I took a picture next to the Luas track with the caption, 'It took me eight years to get here, some might say that was a long Luas journey!' That Luas had taken me to GAA clubs and even court cases, but here I was at the final stop: Dublin's O2 Arena.

I slept like a baby that night and felt great. I was the first fight on the main card, so the bus collected me from the hotel at 3pm, with my fight due to be finished as early as 5pm. That suited me perfectly. 'I get to fight somebody, win, and then watch the biggest UFC event in Ireland ever. And sit wherever I bloody want to!' I went for lunch in a nice place called the Green Room, but the waitress kept looking at me strangely. People's preconceptions were something I had become used to, often having to pay for my food upfront.

'I'm not going to run away,' I assured her. 'I'm going to pay.'

'You're one of the fighters from across the road, aren't you?' she asked. 'This one is on me today.' I was shocked, and although a relatively small gesture, it taught me about how far I'd come. I was used to being rejected at the doors of these places, but now they were wishing me luck in the form of free food. My life was changing at this point, and I was being recognised more and more. I enjoyed the look on people's faces when they saw me. In their head, I was a madman. They could not comprehend the thought of getting into a cage to fight another man. It was a different kind of toughness, and I understood why some people became fans and others became fighters. We all have our own stories, our own motivations that prepare us for that special kind of warfare. I loved dealing with the unknown.

As the fight drew nearer, my old friend turned up again and my mindset changed. 'Who does this muppet Josh Sampo think he is?' the Hooligan asked me. 'He's flown all the way over here to take you out in your own town, to make a fool of you. And you're going to let it happen?' The internal battle with my alter ego was always my first duel on fight day. That dark psyche took hold and I found myself shadow-boxing around the room. Sharp and loose, but calm. I could see every shot. I was ready to sprint all the way to the cage and plant my flag, my country's flag, right in the centre. The Hooligan almost bullied me into a deeper mindset, one of anger and motivation, revving me up for the fight. I felt like I could sprint through 100 walls for 100 miles and no one would fucking stop me. It felt like we were headed for war, only I knew I wasn't going to be a casualty on this particular day. I was ready to risk it all, for my son, for the Holohan name, and for my country.

I chose James Gallagher to be in the dressing room with me because I wanted to give him a taste of what the fight night experience would be like. That moment, I believe, planted a seed in him that would grow and grow and make him want that life even more. Once he got a taste of the glitz and opportunity that this level of the game offered, I knew he would run directly towards it. Clive Staunton was there too, having been with me over the years and helping me in so many ways. An amazing coach, an even better friend. And then, of course, John was with me. He was going to have a long day too with so many of our team fighting.

We warmed up in the dressing room, pushing the mats up against the wall. My movement was so fluid and I grew in confidence. We practised wrestling rounds because I knew Sampo was going to try to take me down.

'When you hit him, be careful,' John reminded me. 'He's going to try to take you down. When you get the guard, work your jiu-jitsu.' People often ask about how important a coach's advice and guidance is on the night of a fight, and for me, John's work during the warm-up was always hugely valuable. During these moments, my mind always went into overdrive, trying to compute all kinds of mad situations, but John helped to stop that. I needed someone to back me up, make me beat a jab, make me strike. John blocked out the noise. Instead of my mind doing cartwheels, he kept me chilled and relaxed. When John was in my dressing room and fully focused, I always performed to my best.

Those last five minutes directly before the walk always filled me with excitement, but anxiety too. For some fights I wanted it to be longer, other fights I wanted it to be shorter, and the madness of those five minutes always led to strange thoughts. What song did I choose? Will it go down well? Should I use the toilet? Should we just walk now? Then all of a sudden, the door opened again and it was time to make the walk. I was under no illusions as to how important this moment was. I could see people scattered around the arena, my people. I could see my teammate Cathal. We had worked so hard to get to this moment and it was my time to make the walk. I was the one who could become the first Irishman to get a UFC victory on Irish soil, and there was no way I was going to let the opportunity pass. I was the 'Berserker', a nickname Conor had given me. Berserkers were Norse warriors who fought with uncontrolled ferocity, and I loved that nickname. I was always the guy ready to do whatever it fucking took to get the victory. I could see Sampo trying to catch my eye from across the way, but I didn't want to even acknowledge his existence. I had a job to do and wanted him to feel horrible. With the tricolour clenched in my hand and Hooligan written across my chest, it was time to show the world who I really was.

'Take these last two minutes in, Paddy,' John whispered. 'These are the last two minutes that your life is ever going to be normal.'

'Ten Thousand Hours' blared around the O2. I've always found it hard to describe the feeling of the crowd and the energy it gave me. It was like standing next to a massive speaker and

At Dublin Zoo on a trip with Barnardos children's charity at four or five years of age. I was full of energy as a kid and afraid of nothing.

My big sister Marguerite and I. Five months after this photo was taken, I was in Beaumont Hospital fighting for my life. It very easily could have ended up becoming the last photo ever taken of me.

My mother and I in our garden in Dromcarra, Carra Avenue. I don't know how she did what she did for me, but she's the strongest woman I know.

SUNDAY WORLD, October 5 1997

This little boy walked the five miles home alone from hospital

Making headlines way before I hit the UFC. This was the day I escaped from Our Lady's Children's Hospital in Crumlin and made the three-hour walk home. (© *Independent News and Media*)

The trip to Florida organised by my Aunt Margaret and Uncle Paul. I wouldn't be the person I am today without the two of them. They are my guardian angels.

My uncle Paul, cousin Stephanie and cousin Paul in Waterworld in Florida. That whole trip felt like I was in a dream. My uncle has always had my back and still does to this day.

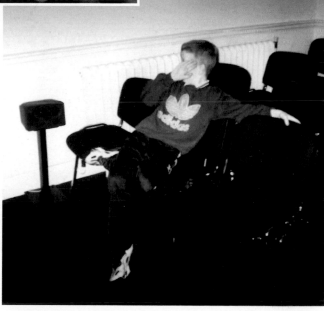

The day my mother got married. I was heartbroken and felt very alone that day.

I scraped together every penny I could and made it to Vegas for the TUF trials. I was the only Irishman trying out and travelled with my mate Adam. His support was something I'll never forget.

After a win in the National Basketball Arena in Tallaght with my sister, Mags.

I took this photo in Vegas while cornering for Ais at the TUF finale. I stared at that photo in the build-up to a lot of my fights – a keyhole into what the fighter sees.

Me and Owen Roddy after selling out Cage Contender and getting the job done in style. Owen beat Shannon Gugerty and I submitted Atremij Sitenkov that night. (*Courtesy of Ciarán Maher*)

Tiernan was like my energy source and leaving for training and fights was always so difficult. This moment shows my scar from brain surgery and also my child, almost like an eerie reminder of my youth.

UFC Dublin. The crowd erupted as I had just sent Josh Sampo to the canvas with an uppercut. I surged forward for the kill and it would have taken an army to stop me that night. All Irish fighters went undefeated. (© *Josh Hedges/Zuffa LLC / Getty Images*)

In Boston vs Shane Howell. I felt invincible that night. Shane was tough but this was my best performance of the year by far. I set my eyes on the prize and fired my weapons with my mind. (© *Ramsey Cardy / SPORTSFILE / Getty Images*)

Nova Scotia, Canada. After I experienced my first official loss. Lola and Kamil are with me in the form of two small love hearts on my shorts. (© *Nick Laham/ Zuffa LLC/Zuffa LLC / Getty Images*)

To carry the Irish flag and to be aware of the weight and expectation it carries is a special feeling. I wore that tricolour like armour and with pride. Thank you to all of the Irish fans – they always energised me. (© *Ramsey Cardy / SPORTSFILE / Getty Images*)

TD Garden, Boston. Backstage with Conor. I had just weighed in, while he waited his turn. We are all lost in our own thoughts, as SevereMMA captures the footage. (© *Mike Roach / Zuffa LLC / Getty Images*)

Boston. Drinking expensive whiskey with Conor. We owe this man a lot. During a recession, he lifted a nation's spirit. His determination and belief instilled confidence in all of us that we could become much more than we ever believed. He was the General. (© *Jeff Bottari / Zuffa LLC / Getty Images*)

After a tough roll in the Concorde Gym. We always shared a mutual respect. (© *Gingerbeard Photography*)

I truly believed that the UFC's issue with my blood condition would be sorted and that I could continue my career with the weight off my shoulders. I continued to prepare for UFC Rotterdam with a training camp in Mjolnir MMA in Iceland. That place was a battleground for Vikings and Celts, all preparing for war together. (*Courtesy of Mjolnir MMA*)

Cheap cans in a secret lagoon in Iceland. I had announced my retirement the day before and it was nice to be surrounded by good people. I wasn't sad, yet. At that time, I was grateful for my life. (*Courtesy of Mjolnir MMA*)

SUBSET painted this mural on the side of a shop facing my grandfather's old house. The shop caused me huge anxiety as a kid. It was the point between all of the roads and if you were caught alone, it often led to a beating. I would sit in my grandfather's parlour for hours, listening to him speak about history, filling my young head with knowledge while we watched the world go by.

On an adventure with Tiernan and Chelsea in the Dublin mountains. My grandad showed me many hidden gems in that area, and I passed on the tradition by showing them to my son.

My mother and Tiernan at his First Communion. I had come a long way from the time my mother walked me there to make my own Communion, and despite not being religious, the moment meant a lot to me.

This was taken after I had beaten Dave Roche in a grappling match in Drogheda. We had many differences but decided to settle them like men. This picture will tell one hundred stories in ten years' time.

My first love of fighting is the ability to teach others and see their faces light up. It's our duty as humans to help develop the generations coming after us. (*Courtesy of Ailish Nicholson*)

John asked me to post this picture days after I decided to leave the Tallaght gym. The people of Tallaght were voicing their anger and demanding John support my decision. I wanted us to move forward together, but John did not comment or share the post afterwards. I slept in Dublin Airport car park that night after cornering a fight up north and then flew to Liverpool to corner Richie Smullen.

Jobstown. The election trail was tough. It gives me great pride to walk through the area I grew up in as someone the kids look up to. Today's diversity is inspiring and the experience of watching Jobstown develop will always stay with me.
(© *Independent News and Media*)

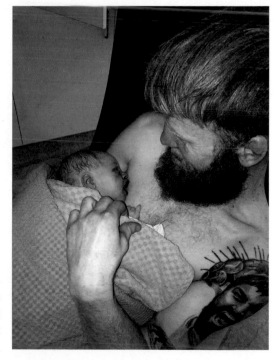

Skin-on-skin with my son Séamus seconds after he was born. I could feel his heart synchronise with mine from that moment on.

My family at the Hellfire Club in the Dublin Mountains – our favourite place to walk. I have overcome many mountains of my own while pacing through these ones.

being able to inhale every single beat. I'm not religious, but it felt like my grandfather was there looking down on me proudly that night. I could feel his presence. Even my own body, it felt like I wasn't the one controlling it, that I was above everything looking down. Before I knew it, I was at the door of the cage. The cage was something of a paradox for me throughout my mixed martial arts career. While the natural reaction for people is to feel restricted in a locked cage, for me it was the opposite. When the cage door swung closed, I felt at my most free. I didn't have to think about the stresses of life, the financial worries, providing for my family. Thoughts of my blood condition were left back in Jobstown, stuffed away in my bedroom locker with the rest of the fucked-up stuff I'd been through in my short life. Being in that cage felt natural to me. Locking out the world. I was the warrior and this was my battleground.

I looked across at Josh and he was clearly in fight mode too. The entire arena was heaving from side-to-side like the *Titanic*, but this time, there was only one person going down, and I was the ginger iceberg ready to sink anything in my way. We touched gloves and the fight was on. I was calm at the start, composed and trying not to rush in. I faked with the jab, and then a little exchange occurred, before he pushed me to the fence. I did pretty well and got to my underhook before wrestling for a little and separating. Time was passing and the cheers of 'Olé', Olé, Olé' began to fill the arena. Each one gave me more and more energy. I looked over at Sampo and he was even singing along, but that infuriated me.

'This has nothing to do with you.'

I came forward and launched jab after jab. Then I faked a jab and noticed he started to do the same thing each time, covering up, but waiting for the right moment to throw the shot. I showed him the uppercut and he just ducked down. I had a full read on him. I faked again, skipped in with my back leg and then unleashed an unmerciful uppercut that would have uprooted a tree. Boom! I connected perfectly with his chin and he immediately fell on top of me, but I brushed him off and Sampo dropped backwards like a fallen door. People said they were shocked that I had dropped him like that with an uppercut, and I can guarantee there was no one as shocked as I was when I saw him smash off the canvas. I felt supernatural, like I could shoot him with my fists. I jumped on top and started to hit him through the guard. I was just about to win my first ever UFC fight and in some style, but all of a sudden, I felt a pain shoot through my hand, as if it was caught in a machine. Sampo grabbed a kimura grip and spun under. I could feel the tension on my arm tightening and knew I was in big trouble. I quickly jumped around to the far side of his head but it was no good, my elbow popped. The pain almost brought me to my knees, but I couldn't stop. I found myself on his back but my arm felt like it was broken, and I knew if we ended up standing again, I was fucked. I had to finish him straight away. I was a purple belt at the time, and Sampo was a brown belt, so I wasn't just going to be choking out any amateur, but I somehow locked in the rear naked choke without using my sore hand and cranked it tighter and tighter with every bit of strength I had left. Once locked in, there was only going to be one outcome. Sampo tapped immediately.

Never in my life had I felt such a surge of relief, emotion, and achievement through the act of one man tapping. I was respectful, but just wanted to celebrate on my own. I had a trick up my sleeve for that Dublin crowd and one that I knew they'd enjoy. I wanted to pay tribute to the influence that Robbie Keane had on me and so many other Jobstownians, so I pulled out his famous cartwheel celebration and shot an imaginary arrow into the air, straight up at my grandad. The crowd loved that one. The place was on fire and there was alcohol flying through the air, drops landing on me. I felt like I was in a dream.

John ran over and gave me great advice. 'Make sure you give Ais props for being in The Ultimate Fighter.' Ais had got the call for the latest series and I missed having her in my corner that night. She had helped me throughout my whole career and I would have loved for her to be there on my biggest night. The microphone made its way over to me and I wasn't worried about bigging myself up, I wanted to take this moment and make it about my teammate. It showed how close we all were back then.

'Ais, I know you're out there in The Ultimate Fighter house, keep your head up. We're out here, we're working for you and we're coming to take this whole game over.' I didn't know it then, but that moment meant everything to her. When the TV episode finally aired, there was a moment where it cut to me and then to Ais in the house and she was bawling crying, inconsolable. 'I was having the worst week of my life, and that moment just brought me up, Paddy,' she told me. Before the interview finished, I was asked about how I felt and what I wanted to do next. I only wanted one thing.

'Man, I just want a cup of tea.'

I walked out of the cage, a different life awaiting me. I went backstage through the handshakes and hugs, and before I even showered I went into the room where I would get paid. I got $8,000 for turning up for the fight and another $8,000 for the victory. Some fighters say that the money doesn't come into their head, but for me, it was the opposite. I was fixated on my earnings, I needed that money for my family. When I got the cheques, covered in blood and sweat, I burst into tears.

Thankfully, the UFC paid in two normal-sized cheques and not those oversized novelty ones you see on TV. I'd have been in more danger walking through Dublin with two of them than I'd ever have been stepping into a cage.

It was history in the making, us versus them. I headed back to the dressing room and the lads arrived for their fights.

'Did we score?'

'Yeah, Paddy banged one in. It's 1-0.'

My victory was significant for a number of reasons, but one of them was definitely in the betting stakes. Every second person in the crowd must have been clutching their betting slips after backing me at 6/1 for a 1st Round Submission victory. If things went well for the rest of the evening, it would be a tough night for the bookmakers. I didn't know anything about betting, but after my victory, we had all made some money; me from the UFC, and half of my estate from the bookies.

Backstage, I showered and got my stuff together. It was difficult to comprehend what I had achieved. I didn't own a suit at the time and that was something I would regret, particularly when I was called to the press conference later that evening with Conor. All I had was an SBG T-shirt and a pair of tracksuit bottoms that I had gotten a lend of. Even Josh Sampo had a suit.

I couldn't wait to see Tiernan. I went down to a side door to see my mates. As I was making my way out, the doors on the elevator slid open. I put down the phone. 'Dana White is in front of me, I'll call you back.'

'What's the story, Dana?' I said and reached over to shake his hand. He had just tweeted that Paddy Holohan blew the roof off the O2 Arena and my phone was blowing up.

'Paddy Holohan! I'm going to make you a rich man. I'll see you at the press conference.' I remember foolishly thinking to myself that I was going to get the $50,000 Performance of the Night bonus. My mind was doing cartwheels and maths at the same time, wondering what to spend the money on. I remember when Conor won the 'Sixty Gs, baby!' in Stockholm and I thought he was sorted for life. Now I was going to get the same. Unfortunately, it didn't work out that way in the end, but it was good to see Gunni, Cathal and Conor get bonuses. At the press conference, Conor even joked to Dana.

'Are you going to give Paddy one?'

Dana turned around and said, 'Give him half of yours, Conor!'

'Ah no, fuck that,' Conor said. I had to laugh.

After meeting Dana at the elevator, the security guard led me over to see my friends. It was towards the side of the arena near a quiet bar with a balcony and everyone who I cared about was there, but it didn't take long for me to get noticed. It got weird real quick. Was I famous now? My mate Macker brought me out with him and we ended up sitting in the crowd. Cathal had won his fight and I was delighted that all his hard work had paid off. Neil Seery was in the cage too having a tough dust-up with Phil Harris and I was cheering them on in my borrowed T-shirt and tracksuit bottoms, but people soon noticed who I was so I had to leg it again.

I walked up to the back row and a lad handed me a cup of tea. 'Here you go, Paddy, but that will be €2.' I didn't have a penny in my pockets, so some random guy next to me paid for it. I had just made $16,000 but still had to get €2 off a randomer for a cup of tea. I went back up to the dressing room where I had stashed my cheques, and got my stuff ready. Conor's moment was approaching, so I met him in the dressing room, shook his hand and wished him the best of luck. I went back downstairs, sat next to one of the medical lads cageside, and watched Gunni get the victory too. It was amazing and looked set to be an unforgettable night for Irish MMA. If people thought myself and the other lads had pressure on our shoulders to deliver in front of this crowd, one can only imagine the weight of expectation on Conor. Everyone had won their fights and it was now up to him. He was the main event in front of a hometown crowd in only his third UFC fight and up against a tough guy in Diego Brandao, who had won The Ultimate Fighter. Additionally, everyone's betting accumulators were resting on a Conor victory and he had the potential to make a lot of people rich that night, including himself. The man walked out like a general, ready to deliver. Nothing ever fazed him. The atmosphere in the place lifted another few levels for Conor's walkout, and I could fully appreciate how big a moment this was set to be. Not just for Conor, not just for me, but for all of us. For Irish MMA. We were on the brink of history that night and it would have taken an army to stop us.

At the first exchange, I could see that Conor had gotten into Diego's head. He was an expert at psychological warfare and had already secured victory in that department the day before the fight. After the weigh-in, we had gone back up to the press conference room. While we were sitting there, Conor kept picking and nibbling at Diego, saying all kinds of things to him until finally Diego snapped. The Brazilian jumped out of his seat and launched a bottle of water across the room at Conor, lid still on it, and nearly hit him. Brandao was lucky it missed because with the mindset we were in, Ireland versus the rest, he wouldn't have made it out of the room that day. Conor, to his credit, stayed as calm as ever. He leaned down, picked up

the bottle of water and took a sip — 'Thank you, Diego!' —
the perfect dose of calm in the chaos of combat, something
Conor was a master at. It wouldn't be the last time Conor was
involved in a bottle-throwing incident, but he was completely
in control. It was a moment of weakness from the Brazilian. We
knew Conor was in his head and under his skin, and it showed
on fight night. And just like that, Conor strolled into the cage,
knocked Brandao out in the first round and wrote our names
into Irish MMA folklore.

The place was heaving from side to side, ready to explode, a
tsunami of gargle tumbling down the crowd. Then Conor got
on the microphone and uttered those famous words that he
had forged in Iceland. 'We're not here to take part, we're here to
take over.' That sentence was like a detonator, it blew the entire
place into smithereens. Conor's punches were strong but his
punchlines often did the most damage. It took a small group
of very brave lads to go in there and represent our country and
show them that we're here to stay, that Irish MMA had to be
taken seriously. We paved the way for future generations, just
like the likes of Tom King and Clive Staunton paved the way
for us. Everyone had a job to do and everyone delivered 100%.

The crowd eventually started to make their way out of the
arena but I didn't want to leave. I wanted that moment to last
for ever. I took hundreds of photos with fans that night. My
life had changed in an instant, but it had taken an eternity to
get to that position. We went back to the dressing room and
it was just calm. John, Conor, Cathal and I standing in there,
taking a breath and trying to fully appreciate the magnitude of
what we had just achieved. We took a selfie and John posted it
online. From that moment onwards, a day didn't pass without
someone messaging me online.

We'll probably never see the likes of that night again. It was one of those nights that was the culmination of years of tough graft on cold winter nights, and thousands of hours. People might try to recreate it but there will never be another night like UFC Fight Night 46 in Dublin. The bus arrived at the arena to drop us back to our hotel, but there was no way I was leaving out the back entrance. I put my bag on my shoulders and walked towards the door. Every time I turned a corner, more people recognised me but I didn't care. I walked the streets of Dublin with pride.

When I got back to the hotel room, I closed the door and took another deep breath, looking at myself in the mirror. Everything had changed in a day but I was still me, still Paddy Holohan from Jobstown. I plugged in my phone and the wave of messages just kept coming and coming. Beep, beep, beep. It was like Morse code coming through my phone. Everything maxed out, including the memory on my phone. That night we went to Lillie's Bordello in Dublin's city centre for a few drinks but I couldn't move. It was too packed. Everyone had gone their own way and I was wrecked emotionally and physically so didn't stay out too long.

When I drove to the O2 Arena earlier in the week to collect my stuff, I drove there in a black 1998 Toyota Avensis, but it was clamped when I parked on the path outside. If I hadn't splashed my per diem on three pairs of runners, I probably would have been able to afford to remove the clamp. I just had to leave it there and get the Luas home. A few days after the fight, I went back to get it but it was gone and I never saw it again. I got a loan of a friend's car, put on 50 Cent's 'Straight to the Bank' and headed off to cash my UFC cheques. When the money landed, I bought myself a second-hand Volvo S40 and asked my mother what she wanted.

'Anything you want, Ma? I'm rich now.'

'Do you know what I want, son? I'd love a chrome bin.'

A €60 bin and that was it, she was delighted. I brought Tiernan shopping and held his hand as he picked out a new tracksuit and a pair of runners. For the first time, I felt like I was able to provide for my family. Conor gave me strong advice, 'Don't go broke trying to act rich,' and that stuck with me throughout my career. I was the only father out of us all and knew the responsibility that came with being someone's dad. I had no choice but to be clever with my money. I began to think about the future. Things had changed, but we just didn't know it yet.

Another of Conor's pieces of wisdom was that 'money doesn't change people, it reveals them,' and that would certainly ring true as time passed. Some people just weren't made for the pressure that comes with being in the limelight, the stress of everyone thinking you have so much money, and the attention that comes with it. Some people's view of themselves and the worth of others can be changed by money. The way to live life is to excel and launch yourself into the stars, fulfilling your potential without having to put other people down. I didn't become a fighter to make others feel bad or to think less of themselves. Fame meant nothing to me. It was about legacy, and a positive one at that. I wanted to head for the stars and take as many people as possible with me. I wanted to give more than I take from this life.

Paddy Holohan, 10-0 — July 2014

Round 3

CHAPTER 11 ....

Winning at UFC Dublin was the greatest night of my career, without a doubt, but there was one person who was missing.

Kamil Rutkowski was more than just a teammate. He was my friend. The two of us started out in SBG around the same time and came up through the ranks together. Kamil was a bull of a man and such a great training partner, but he also had a soft and kind side. He used to work in the SuperValu in Tallaght and would pick up my mother and bring her and her groceries home whenever he saw her. My ma would usually be really suspicious of people, but she loved Kamil.

We were friends, but I never knew how badly Kamil was struggling. One day after training, John came over to me at reception.

'Listen, you need to go try to find Kamil,' he said. 'He's not well. If you find him, I need you to bring him to Beaumont Hospital.'

Kamil had been in the office the previous day but there was something unusual in his behaviour that had John worried, and he wanted me to bring Kamil to a doctor to check him out.

'He hasn't been acting like himself,' John said. 'Something isn't right.'

When I got to Kamil's house, his car wasn't there but his little Jack Russell was and that immediately put me on alert. I got back into my car and my gut told me to go towards Massey's Woods, an old estate in the Dublin mountains. I had seen Kamil posting pictures from there a few days earlier, strange pictures of himself alone, staring down the camera with a dark look on his face. When I arrived, I could see his car. It was empty. My heart sank.

I didn't know what to do. 'Maybe you should go get help,' I thought to myself. I didn't know if I would find Kamil, and if I did, how he would react.

'Kamil! Kamil!' I shouted, walking down the lane and deeper into the woods, but he was nowhere to be seen. It was a vast wooded area, and it was clear I wasn't going to find him by myself. I went back down the mountains to call Kamil's brother, Rafael, and tell him I had found Kamil's car. When I drove back up to Massey's an hour later, there was a Garda car parked up on the road. My heart sank even further. His car was still there.

'Garda, did you find a body in there?' I asked, resigned to the fact that Kamil was in serious trouble.

'No, has something happened?' The Gardaí didn't know that Kamil was missing. They were there to deal with a group of young lads on quad bikes. Maybe I was overreacting? He hadn't been missing that long. I had already started my training camp for the Dublin card, so I decided to head back down again and go for a quick run. It would help me think clearly, and after that, I'd collect Kamil's brother and the two of us could go back to look through the woods together. As I was driving past The Square in Tallaght, my phone rang. It was Kamil's brother, and I knew immediately from the sound of his voice it was something bad.

'He's dead, Paddy. He's dead.'

'What do you mean he's dead?'

'He's dead. He killed himself.'

'Where are you? I'll come find you.'

I couldn't believe it. Kamil was gone. I went back to the forest, and a group of people had already gathered. I made my way over to the spot and there he was, on the bank of a hill. That sight will never leave me. Just a few days earlier, he had been with us. Now he was gone, permanently.

When Kamil died, it changed everything. His death broke everyone, so many strong people unable to cope with the devastation. That day changed me. I was empty. Numb. I couldn't cry. The only emotion I could feel was anger. I thought of Izzy, my old friend who had taken his life when we were younger. I tormented myself. I should have spent longer in the forest looking for him. How could we have been so close to Kamil, but not know that he was going through this suffering and pain on the inside? The Monday before it happened, I had been training with Kamil. We were rolling and I caught him in a submission. He turned around, looked me dead straight in the eyes and smiled.

'You will never catch me like that again,' he said.

In that moment, I thought it was such a strange thing for him to say, so out of character, and the more I thought about it, the more I wondered if he had already decided that he was going to end his own life. We never knew the pain he was in.

I spent time with Kamil's brother afterwards, helping him to get stuff ready for the coffin and plaques to commemorate his life before his body was repatriated to be buried in Poland. We held a memorial in SBG, and Kamil was awarded his black belt posthumously. It was a lovely moment. I know he would have been proud.

I really struggled to deal with Kamil's death. I tried to deal with my anger, my grief, all of my emotions by myself. I still hadn't come to terms with losing Kamil when Lola, my ex-girlfriend, took her own life as well.

Lola wasn't just a girl who I had been seeing when I was younger. I loved her, and she loved me. We had so much history together. We argued, we cried, we kissed. We did things that only the two of us would ever know about, little things that only we shared. But then our relationship had gone from being inseparable to nuclear, and eventually, back to being tolerable again. I couldn't escape the guilt I felt about how things ended up between us. In truth, once things fell apart, our lives took different turns and we didn't see much of each other.

Not long before the UFC Dublin card, I had met up with Lola for a cup of coffee and it was great to sit together and talk, just the two of us. I had heard she wasn't doing too well and I still cared about her deeply. The trauma of that horrific night when she was attacked was as painful as ever for her, I felt. She was really struggling with her mental health, going in and out of hospital following a series of nervous breakdowns. That day when we met, she was quiet and seemed very down.

A few weeks later, my phone rang and her brother Dave's name flashed up on the screen. I knew why he was calling and it cut me like a knife. Lola had been talking about taking her own life and earlier that day, I got a phone call to say that she had gone missing and her family were fearing the worst. I answered.

'Paddy, Lola's dead,' Dave told me, and I broke down immediately. I just couldn't understand what had happened, couldn't comprehend the fact that Lola saw death as her only escape. I was heartbroken. My head filled with so many negative thoughts. Could I have done something to help her? I remember asking her brother, 'Dave, did she say anything?', searching for answers to an unsolvable tragedy. The invincibility I felt after winning at UFC Dublin was a distant memory, and all of those horrible, anxious emotions of the past that I had fought came rushing back. It's a strange feeling; being happy that the person is out of their misery, but being utterly distraught that they've taken their life. I stood there at her funeral, numb, unable to cry. I miss Lola and I always will. I just hope she's at peace now.

In the weeks after Lola's funeral, I found myself running down to her grave. I could be out jogging but get a sudden urge to change my route and head straight for her grave. There was a tap near the grave, and I'd take a drink and spend some time there, just the two of us, before heading off on my run again. One day, I was standing at Lola's grave and my phone rang. It was John, but I ignored the call. I had become disillusioned with life, so negative, that I felt he could only be calling me to say that the UFC had finally found out about my blood disorder. There I was, standing in the graveyard, thinking that my career was over, and I couldn't even shed a tear. I left the graveyard, gathered myself, and decided to bite the bullet and ring John back. I was right, the UFC had called him, but it was good news.

'Do you want to fight in Canada?' he asked me. 'In Nova Scotia?' A minute earlier, I thought my career was over. Now here I was with another UFC fight. I breathed a sigh of relief and agreed straight away.

Getting back into a fight camp was the perfect antidote to all the emotional difficulties I had been trying to deal with. I was surrounded by tragedy and I needed something positive to channel my energy towards. There was so much going on in the gym that I had to organise the sparring myself, but that didn't bother me. Cathal and Gunni were booked to fight in Sweden around the same time and I wanted to prove to the world that we, SBG, could fight in two different countries at the same time and still come out victorious. It was the next step for the progression of Irish MMA. Divide and conquer.

For my training camps, I had 'Team Midget' — a group of us in the gym who were all around the same size, Alex Brophy, Aisling Daly, Richie Smullen. John wouldn't be travelling to Nova Scotia with me, but we did do some one-on-one sessions together ahead of my fight. I don't know if John spent more time with me because he knew that I was going through a tough time. I wasn't used to getting that attention from him, but my star was rising and the attention surrounding me was too.

The camp went well. We had arranged that Artem would go out to Las Vegas for Conor's fight with Chad Mendes, and then would fly up to me in Nova Scotia. He would help with one side of my corner on fight night and Ais would do the other. We were inexperienced but I didn't want to let negative thoughts seep into my preparation. Excuses were not welcome.

Five days out from the fight my opponent, Louis Gadinot, pulled out of the fight and a local fighter called Chris Kelades stepped up to take his place. From the outside looking in, you might think that an opponent who only has five days' notice is nothing to worry about, but that's the wrong mindset. If the UFC is coming to your town, and you can see that there are about seven fighters on the card in your weight class, the likelihood is that one of them is going to pull out and you need to be ready for the call. Kelades was a smart guy and had an 8-1 record. He was a preacher too, and that made me see myself as a sort of pagan; 'The Pagan v the Pastor' is what I called it. The overall experience of Nova Scotia was amazing — I learned the history of the town and how the Irish had emigrated there years ago — but I knew I was in for a knock. The fact that I was Irish didn't matter; the entire town had turned on me in support of their preacher.

The weight cut didn't go well. The night before the weigh-in, I dripped out all of my water and ended up lying there soaking in my bed, heavily dehydrated. I got to the weigh-in and I was so angry, pacing around backstage while Kelades just stood there relaxed. I got onto the stage and I knew instantly it was a case of them against me. Even the local UFC commissioner, a Canadian, pulled me aside beforehand. 'You better not touch him out there,' he warned me. 'Keep your hands to yourself.'

I grabbed my flag, stood on the scales and let out a scream, the type that would usually send the crowd wild, but it was met with crickets. I had come from mayhem in Dublin to this sorry excuse of a weigh-in with the atmosphere of a wake. At that moment, all I wanted was a shot of adrenalin from the fans, but there was hardly anyone there. It made me realise the value that we, the Irish, were giving the UFC too. We were the big draw, not these unknown lads. I leaned right into Kelades' face but it was no use. He just leaned back and laughed, and maybe I should have done the same. I should have just chilled out. I always felt like any fight could be my last one so the idea of not turning it into something massive was alien to me. My attitude was to set fire to the building, see what happens, and allow the madness to take over.

Later that evening, I found an amazing lobster restaurant down by the sea. I told Artem and Ais to order whatever they wanted, and we all tucked into $80 lobsters.

'Paddy, slow down! Slow down! That's a week's shopping,' I thought to myself. I was set to make $20,000 if I won this fight, but it had already cost me $2,000 to fly Artem up from Vegas, which the UFC had taken out of my purse, as well as another $2,000 for food and travel out there, minus 15 per cent tax. All of a sudden, it felt like I was fighting for buttons.

I slept okay the night before the fight but I let out my water again, soaking the bed. The next morning, I walked around the town looking for Pedialyte, which would help to prevent dehydration, and a gumshield. People were catching my eye at the traffic lights and I would react with, 'What the fuck are you looking at?' I went into a shop that sold gumshields.

'We're all out,' the guy behind the counter said, clearly lying to me.

'I can see loads of them behind you.'

'No, none of those would fit you.'

It felt like the whole town was definitely against me now. I still couldn't shake the feeling of dehydration. I took the UFC bus to the arena and went into the dressing room and a negative thought entered my mind: 'This should be easy. I get to fight in the UFC against a guy who's only had a few days' notice.' I should have slapped myself on the wrists right there and then for even allowing that kind of thought. We were in Kelades' hometown and I should have known there was no way he would make it easy.

When the time to walk finally came, I could tell that my corner were really nervous. I could see it on Ais's face. Throughout my career, I took every opportunity I could to corner a fight because I knew it was all experience that would make me a better coach long term. It allowed me to understand what worked with different types of people. Before the fight, Artem said to me, 'Listen, I'm not a cornerman, I'm just here to support you, Paddy,' and I respected that. Artem was the type that would only need a bottle of water and still go out and fight well, whereas I was different. I needed a person in my corner to relax me, to talk me through certain situations, but in Nova Scotia, about to walk out for my second-ever UFC fight, I was nervous about them being nervous. We got to the door, and I walked out to 'Superheroes' by The Script. It suited me so much in my head but was completely flat when I walked out. The atmosphere was completely dead, but as soon as the cage door swung shut, I felt great again. Angry, but in a good way.

I threw everything at Kelades in that first round and it was close to perfect. I should have started a little slower and more calmly, but I was trying to head-kick, leg-kick and take him down all at the same time. It was a great fight, back and forward. He smashed me in the face with an elbow, and I just went, 'Whoa, that was fucking hard.' I smashed him with a right hand, and he returned fire with a right of his own, and we both went backwards. I was eventually able to take his back, but Kelades was saved by the buzzer. We got to the end of the first round, and I felt like I had dominated it. I strode to the corner confidently, knowing I was one up.

The second round began and Kelades started strongly right out of the gates. There was a moment where I took him down, got on his back, controlled him, but then there were times he caught me with knees in the chest and I could feel my stamina waning. There was even a moment I was in a double leg and I just remember looking at the crowd and letting out a breath: 'God, I can't wait for this one to be over.' I should never have been thinking like that. I would usually be firing on all cylinders, but I wasn't myself.

I fought well in the second round, apart from one instance where I made a crucial mistake and Kelades capitalised by mounting me. He just kept punching me over and over, and I could feel every shot striking my face and knocking my head from side to side. I had no choice but to start fighting from the bottom, something I would never advise, but it kept the fight going. The referee needed me to do something, and I was left with no option. Kelades switched to an armbar but somehow I held on. I made it to the buzzer at the end of the round, but I'd had to endure a hard thirty or forty seconds of eating shots. I climbed to my feet and stumbled into the side of the cage.

'Artem, the stool, the stool,' I could hear Ais screaming. I didn't really know what was going on, but I got the feeling Ais might have thought the fight was over. The commissioner came over and inspected me so I shook myself a bit and got it together but there was no sign of my corner. I was on my own.

I was physically drained and I remember thinking, 'Come on, Paddy. Take a deep breath. Stabilise yourself, lad. Stay loose, focus and finish this man.' Without a sip of water, and with some self-cornering, it was time for round three. I had just been on the deck and now I had to go straight back out again. I put that to the side as best I could and started the third round better than I finished the second. I landed shots, he landed shots. I landed takedowns, he landed kicks, I landed kicks, he landed takedowns. He got me in a choke, but I used my experience of using the same choke on people to fool him into thinking he had locked it in fully. I made a loud choking sound — *kshhhh* — and he started to pull tighter and tighter, but I was fine. It was a clever one that absorbed his energy, and I started to laugh so he had no choice but to let go. That moment was one of the only times I felt like Paddy Holohan again.

The round finished and I dragged myself to my feet. I was physically drained, but thankful when I saw Ais, Artem and the stool waiting for me in my corner. The fight went the distance and I had so much respect for Kelades after an evenly matched battle. I thought I had won, but nothing is ever certain and I ended up losing by unanimous decision. I was devastated, but I also knew it was my own fault for not getting the finish, for allowing it to go to the judges in the first place. As I walked back to the dressing room, the realisation of my loss started to sink in.

'Ha, you Irish douchebag!' some guy shouted from the crowd.

'Say that again, you prick!'

I tried to get over the barrier to get my hands on him but security dragged me away. When I got back to the dressing room, Firas Zahabi came over to me. Firas was the head coach at Tristar Gym in Montreal and he was there with Rory MacDonald, who was fighting in the main event.

'You performed really well, that was good,' Firas told me, 'but here's one piece of advice from my point of view. You just fought, man; you need to build back up. You need to start managing this properly.'

'No, Firas,' I said. 'I need to get paid. I need this.'

'Listen,' he said, 'if you want this to go far, you need to relax. You need to find good management. You could do very well in this game.' Firas didn't have to give me that speech, but I knew he was right. I had fought twice in three and a half months. I was tired and had a lot of shit going on in my life.

I had been through a terrible few months on a personal level, and now this was my first official loss. A short phone call from John to show he cared would have made a huge difference. When Chris Kelades came over to talk to me, I just felt an urge to hug him, looking for any little bit of reassurance. Gunni lost on the same night in Stockholm, so John was dealing with that, but I was one of his generals. I just wanted someone to say, 'Paddy, you're going to be alright after this,' because truly, I didn't know if I was.

John wasn't the reason I lost but it would have meant a lot more for me to die on my sword in front of the man who I had been through so much with. I had put a lot on the line for him over the years. It would have been nice to hear whatever words of comfort he would have had for me in that isolation. When I got back to Dublin, he sent me a text listing the negatives and positives of my performance, and 'win or learn' was about as good as his advice got. I never really believed in that philosophy, that if you learn from your defeats, you will eventually win. The first time I had heard that saying was in a book I read on Nelson Mandela. When John applied it to fighting, I understood how it could work in the gym but not on the battlefield. If I entered any cage with that mindset, I would have already lost. To me, it was come home with your shield or on your shield. That's the way to fight.

'Win or learn' does nothing for the fighter who can't sleep because he's up all night thinking about his loss. 'Win or learn' is something you do in the gym, not on a UFC fight card or in the cage. It just isn't enough. It's never enough. If you keep on learning, you'll just end up getting fed up with learning; the black eyes, the broken noses, the depression from successive losses. My view was to give it absolutely everything, and if I failed after doing that, then that's a loss I can accept. I could never walk towards a situation thinking that if I lost, I'd get a lesson from it. In the cage, there's only room for win. If you want to learn, that should happen in the gym. In the cage, you're going to need to jam that square peg into the round hole with pure will and determination.

The pain of that loss still haunts me, but there was a silver lining later that night. We had gone to the pub and I was sitting there, sipping on a terrible Guinness, wallowing in self-pity.

'You won the bonus, you won the bonus!' Ais screamed. The fight was picked as Fight of the Night, and I'd won a $50,000 bonus. If your '0' has gotta go, you might as well sell it for a nice chunk of cash. I know plenty of people in Ireland who lost their '0' in a GAA club for a €50 Fightshop voucher.

The news of the bonus lifted our spirits, and I walked out of the bar to take a minute to myself. I sat down next to a homeless man outside.

'What's that black eye from?' he asked.

'I've been fighting tonight, but I lost.'

'Oh really? Here, look, do you want something for yourself?' And with that he pulled out a small bag of weed from his pocket.

'That will help.'

I laughed and walked over to a quiet spot. I needed compassion and kindness; I just didn't think it was going to come from a Canadian homeless man. At that moment it was exactly what I needed. I was drug-tested throughout my career. If I was in camp, I was in. But after the disappointment of losing, I didn't even know if being 'in' was what I wanted any more. I sat there, contemplating everything; my career, my life. I had lost, but had earned $50,000. Maybe I needed to be less emotional about everything and accept that I was an entertainer. Maybe I just needed to put everything on the line, entertain people, and make as much money for my family as possible. I thought about everything that night — about Lola, about Kamil — and for a minute, the world stopped.

Paddy Holohan, 10-1 — October 2014

CHAPTER 12 ....

C anada was an equaliser. It allowed me to focus on something other than death and depression, but the fact that it went so badly only forced me into a downward spiral yet again. But, like every tough moment in my life, I did everything I could to just keep ploughing forward. There was huge pressure on me after losing to Chris Kelades in Nova Scotia. My UFC contract was for four fights, and despite only signing it in July, I had already fought twice by October with a third on the horizon. Most UFC fighters wouldn't even comprehend fighting that many times in such a short period, and I still had no idea why I kept accepting fights. Maybe I needed something to keep me focused, to prevent me falling off the tracks.

The UFC can be a cut-throat business and I knew that if I wanted to continue to be a part of it, I needed to win my next fight. The call came when Conor was booked to headline a card in Boston in January 2015. Conor had fought in the TD Garden before, against Max Holloway, and that night showed just how meaningful and profitable the Irish invasion could be for the UFC. I knew they'd go back there, and I knew that if they were going to give me a fight, it would almost certainly be on that card.

'It was fucking mental over there,' Conor told me. 'There were old lads coming up to me trying to speak Gaeilge that had never even set foot in Ireland.' This was music to my ears. I loved our culture and I knew the Boston crowd would strike me with the same bolt of lightning that the Dublin fans had.

The significance of fighting in America was never lost on me. This was the fight capital of the world. Steam coming off the shore, bright lights, yellow taxis. I could visualise it all and that helped me in my training. It had always been a goal of mine to go back and fight there again. The Ultimate Fighter had been a horrible experience, one of the loneliest I'd felt, and I had a responsibility to right those wrongs.

I was booked to fight a guy called Shane Howell, a tough country kid who had fought some good opponents. Going in, I knew he was going to be tough, and that I'd need a spade if I was going to KO him. The weather that Christmas was particularly bad, and that training camp was the coldest of my career. It was difficult to get the bodies into the gym and, despite spending a lot of time training on my own, I was blessed to have Team Midget. I was the leader, and our little team had grown, with Blaine O'Driscoll, Tommy Martin and Dylan Tuke joining Ais, Alex, Richie and me. Even the experienced lads respected the graft and energy being put in by the smaller group down the end of the wall. We called them the 'big lads' — Conor, Cathal, Artem, Chris Fields, Philip Mulpeter and Kiefer Crosbie. Every one of us, big or small, remained close. We were all part of Team SBG. We knew where we came from, and where we wanted to get to.

Christmas Day that year was just another day, and it came and went without a second thought. I was cutting weight over a longer period, which meant that Christmas dinner was a few slices of dry turkey and green vegetables — no potatoes, no salt, not even a drop of gravy. I hadn't smelled a potato in weeks and even considered rubbing a few of them against me just to get some starch into my body. I knew I wasn't suffering alone, though. Conor was fighting at 145lb and had a vicious cut ahead of him, and so did Cathal, but going through it together certainly helped. The wink of an eye, or a nod of the head to Cathal or Conor down the mat, and we knew we had our jobs to do. The Boston card had the potential to be another huge night for the gym and we weren't going to let anything threaten our moment.

A week before we flew out to Boston, I brought Tiernan up to the Hellfire Club, a ruin dating back to the 1700s at the top of a hill in Dublin. As Tiernan got older, the goodbyes only got harder. He was my energy, and just the sight of him gave me power and belief. Pushing heavy sleds in the Irish Strength Institute, the thought of his future gave me the little burst I needed to push the sled faster and for longer. I wanted the balance of doing everything I could to provide for him, but also making sure that I wasn't away for months on end; I needed to be there in person for him too. We sat on a rock together and looked down on the thousands of lights peppering the Dublin skyline. There were a million different things going on underneath those lights and none of them mattered to me. Whatever problems I had in my life, they disappeared for a moment. I took stock of how far I had come, held Tiernan close, and readied myself for another war.

I immediately felt at home in Boston, an oxymoron of a city with its cold air and its warm people. They welcomed us with arms wide open, embraced our Irishness and treated us so well that I wanted to put on a performance to remember. After checking into my room, I took some time to myself and stood outside, inhaling the freezing cold air and watching everyone pass. I still couldn't believe that I was about to fight in a 20,000-

seat arena in Boston. I looked across the road and could see Conor's face plastered across a bin, and then on a passing bus. He was everywhere and it felt like a dream. The realisation of just how far we had come was never lost on me, but neither was the distance we had left to go. And that motivated me.

As the day went on, I started to feel worse and worse. Homesickness had set in and knocked me right off course. I couldn't get Tiernan out of my mind. I phoned Denise and even though things weren't great between us at the time, she agreed to fly over with Tiernan, even putting money towards her own flights. In return, I booked them a hotel and bought jumpers, scarves, woolly hats and gloves and left them at reception for when they checked in to their hotel. I recorded a voice message for Tiernan and asked Denise to record his reaction when he listened to it.

'How do you feel about flying to Boston tomorrow, T? You get to see your dad in the UFC.'

He was still just a nipper and exploded with excitement. Before I knew it, I was back on track. There was no way I could lose in front of my son. I only saw him for a few minutes when they landed in Boston but it meant the world to him, and I only wish he was old enough to understand how much it meant to me.

'I'm going to see my da fighting, I'm going to see my da fighting,' he told strangers on the way to the fight. I was told he slept through half of the fight itself but I couldn't blame him. He was only young and I wasn't the first fight any more, I was moving up the card.

When we went to weigh-in, the atmosphere was similar to weighing in in Dublin, threatening to blow every door in the building straight off the hinges. My weight cut had gone well, so well that I was able to hold a glass of coconut water while on the scales without worrying about the consequences. I could see the green, white and orange, and feel the Irish inside that room, screaming back at me. I scanned the crowd, looking for one pair of eyes in particular, and there he was screaming his heart out. That look on Tiernan's face is something I'll never forget. I weighed in, and walked back to the room where Conor was waiting with Dee.

'Paddy, what's it like out there?' Conor asked me. 'Did you see Tiernan?'

'It's fucking mental, Conor. Tiernan was standing in the front row and I got to see his face.'

'Awh, that's fucking deadly man. I'm delighted.'

Conor was going through a tough cut to get to 145lb and didn't have to ask me about Tiernan, but caring for his friends is what Conor does best. I know him away from the bright lights and left hands, I know him as a human, and he has the same doubts, worries, questions, and feelings as we all do. But he's also got a sharp wit that can cut down the biggest of personalities.

Before the weigh-in, a guy came over to speak with us, trying to act cool. 'I don't know who you are, mate,' Conor said to him, and I burst out laughing, 'He looks melted though, Conor.' I knew exactly who it was.

Later that day after the weigh-in, we headed back towards the bus. As we walked, I could hear Dana White screaming after us. 'Conor, Mickey Rourke wants to meet you properly.'

'Ah, Dana. I've just made weight. I don't care about Mickey Rourke,' Conor replied. It was surreal – a Hollywood actor chasing Conor for a picture. How crazy that would have sounded just a few years ago. Poor Mickey was getting torn apart by Conor, and all he wanted was a picture. I had to laugh. Eventually, Dana and Lorenzo Fertitta, one of the UFC owners, twisted Conor's arm enough that he went back and took a photo with him. People don't truly appreciate the demands placed on fighters during fight week, but I've never seen anyone deal with them as well as Conor does.

When I woke up on fight day, I felt fantastic. It wasn't like Nova Scotia. This time I was sharp. I could feel the energy and knew the support in the arena would be behind me. I was ready to murder Shane Howell and bury him out the back of the arena without a sense of remorse or guilt. I was fighting for Ireland; we all were. We sellotaped the mats to the wall, stuck the tricolours up too, and got ready for battle. Even the security men were second-generation Irish. All we were short was a trad band and a céilí and it would have felt like we were back home.

The time came and I was first to make the walk — 'The Berserker' once again. I entered to 14,000 screaming voices, baying for a bloodbath as I fought to save my UFC career. I threw everything I had at Howell in that first round. I choked him, jabbed him, cranked him and twisted him. Everything was going to plan until I lost concentration for a second. Howell shook me off his back and I was caught in a bad position, stuck there while he landed heavy shots on my face for four or five seconds. When the bell rang he helped me up and with a thick American country accent said, 'C'mon, Paddy, is that all you got?' All I could do was laugh as I headed over to my corner.

I felt great and I stayed in control for the next two rounds but just couldn't get the finish. I threw everything I had at Howell but he was one tough motherfucker. At one point, I threw a kick at him but he caught it and rolled my left ankle badly. Even with all the adrenalin, I could feel the pain. I tried to take the weight off of it but ended up rolling the other ankle, setting off major alarm bells. In a split second, I went from complete domination to hobbling around on two damaged feet. To make things worse, Howell wasn't stupid and drove forward the second he sensed my weakness. I was in unbearable pain but that voice inside my head started barking at me again. I somehow managed to pull off another takedown and put a body triangle on him, but my foot was nearly foot locking myself due to the injured ankle.

'Change to hooks, change to hooks,' John shouted in to me from the side of the cage.

'I have a body triangle on him!' I think John knew at that moment what I was actually saying: 'Look, I can't. My fucking ankles are in bits.' I kept trying but I just couldn't get Howell to tap. At one stage, I even got through on his neck and could feel everything, the softness of his windpipe, every breath becoming a shortening gasp as I cranked it tighter. But he still wouldn't tap, and I respected him massively for that. He was of the breed that would prefer to be knocked out cold than to tap. The fight ended and although it went to the judges, everyone knew who the victor was. Your winner, by unanimous decision, Paddy 'the Hooligan' Holohan.

I grew ten feet when the referee raised my hand. I didn't give a fuck whether it was in the first second or the last round; I was delighted to get the win. I looked around and my name was shooting from side to side on massive screens all across the stadium. I felt invincible, and the pain in my ankles was a distant memory. I got back to the dressing room, washed the blood off, and threw on the new three-piece suit I had bought for the occasion. When I walked outside, the boys were waiting for me.

'Jesus, Paddy, you're busy,' Chris Fields shouted, laughing. 'Court and a fight on the same day?' I didn't care, though. I felt fresh, and had another $20,000 in my pocket courtesy of the Ultimate Fighting Championship. People might have thought we were earning millions but we weren't. I wasn't complaining, but it would have been nice to be able to come back and buy a house with the money. We were still building something at that point and it was all about the collective; building the team, the SBG brand, the people around us. My dream was always to come home and set up an MMA gym, and every fight I had added more weight and credibility to my CV.

The rest of the card was another one of those special nights where I had a front-row seat to watch guys who had come up from nothing deliver on the biggest of stages. History was unfolding in front of our eyes. Conor and I watched together as Cathal won his fight and then, a little bit later, Conor beat Dennis Siver in the main event. After the fight, Conor was with Lorenzo and Dana sipping whiskey, but I declined the offer and went to a back room eating pizza instead. No way I was drinking whiskey on an empty stomach. When we went out to the press conference, I was damn glad that I wore my suit because it would become an iconic moment in our careers. Conor brought a bottle of Midleton Rare whiskey worth €20,000 with him and we toasted a historic night.

'Well, what do we all think of Paddy Holohan, the Hooligan, in his three-piece? Fucking animal,' Conor said, toasting another glass of whiskey. He tore everyone to shreds in that press conference with some of the funniest lines I'd ever heard. Here we were, sipping from a bottle of whiskey worth €20,000, having the time of our lives. Still the same two boyos from Dublin.

Conor invited me out with Lorenzo and Dana that night, but I had to decline. I had other plans; a date with my son. I got the UFC bus to drop me near Tiernan's hotel and I strolled through the streets of Boston. The temperature had dropped to around -15°C, and I had just a three-piece suit and a smile to keep me warm, but I felt happier than ever. I wrapped my arms around Tiernan and held him for as long as I could before it was time for him to head to sleep. Once he had gone to bed, there was no point in me staying in, so I went back out into the city to celebrate another famous night with my SBG teammates. I enjoyed the celebrations but leapt out of bed the next morning as Tiernan and I had our own celebration with cookies and cream ice-cream on the menu.

Paddy Holohan, 11-1 — January 2015

Coming back to Dublin was a wonderful feeling. I had left Ireland with an uncertain future hanging over my head, but winning in Boston put me right back on track and ready to step up another level in the UFC. The win came at a price, though. Shane Howell had been a tough nut to crack and the swelling around my left ankle was getting worse instead of better. A scan showed that I had done a lot of ligament damage. The UFC gives fighters thirty days to report an injury after a fight but given my medical history, there was no way I was risking any needless attention. I said nothing and paid all the medical costs out of my own pocket.

The thought of the UFC discovering my blood condition was something that always haunted me. It wasn't that I was hiding it from them; they just never asked. I didn't want to be in a position where I would have to explain myself. No fighting promotor would ever understand the intricacies of my blood disorder more than me. I lived with it all of my life. There was no specialist in the UFC's medical wing who could relate to it and the minute someone googled 'factor XIII deficiency', they would see that one of the symptoms is an increased risk of internal cranial haemorrhage. I wasn't stupid; there was no way they would take a chance. My career would be over. I wasn't a millionaire and if I had suddenly found myself unemployed overnight, I wouldn't have been able to survive, let alone provide for a family. I earned about $20,000 for beating Howell in Boston and made sure to hold on to as much of it as possible. It looks great as one big number but it quickly disappears after paying for a camp, flights and tax. I was always thinking about life after fighting, and Conor, our general, made sure to reinforce that perspective: get in, get rich, get out. Some people look at fighting in a cage as a circus show, and we're very much the animals.

It was around this time that I had started texting someone new, and I was smitten from the start. I had never met Chelsea in person, didn't know her at all until after the Dublin fight when she sent me a message online to say that she was blown away by the selflessness I had shown by mentioning Ais in my interview.

'I'm not a stalker or mad fan,' she wrote, 'but I just want to let you know that speech you gave for Aisling was inspirational.'

I messaged Chelsea back but I knew I had to be careful. I didn't appear it on the outside but I was actually quite fragile. Growing up, I was always with the wrong people and ended up either getting hurt or hurting them. My warped mind used to think the more relationships you have, the more other people will think of you, but I was so wrong. I missed significant milestones in my life. I never learned the value of being intimate with someone you truly care about. From the moment I started to text Chelsea, things just felt different. Years ago, I kept a law of attraction book, and in it I wrote that I wanted to marry a blonde girl from Merseyside. I had only been texting Chelsea so couldn't hear the distinctive Liverpudlian accent, and it made me even happier when I found out where she was from.

Chelsea had a trip to Dublin planned with her friend for 30 January, two weeks after my Boston fight, so the timing couldn't have been better. We had been texting for so long now that I was excited to finally meet her in person. I didn't usually get nervous with girls but this felt different. I invited Dylan Tuke out with me, and the two of us headed into Dublin city centre. A text came in from Chelsea saying she was at the Old Storehouse in Temple Bar, the last place I wanted to go. It was a tourist trap and if any of the lads saw me and Dylan heading in there, they'd probably think we were two creeps looking to hook up with tourists. I really liked Chelsea, though, so I made an exception. Walking in the doors of the pub, the nerves disappeared. It could have been the few pints I had just gargled, or something deeper, but I was just excited to meet her now. I walked into the room and spotted her immediately, awestruck by her beauty. She was everything I had ever wanted; curly platinum blonde hair, boots up to her knees, and the perfect smile. I made a beeline for Chelsea, shook her hand and just stuck the lips on her right there and then in front of Dylan and her friend. She was shocked, but soon laughed about it.

'Ah, we might as well break the ice,' I said.

We had a wonderful time and hit it off straight away, and agreed to meet again the following day. Dylan was only a teenager and probably still a bit too young, so I decided I'd bring Ruairi, another of my friends, with me on the second night. It turned out to be a terrible decision. If Dylan was a two on the wild scale, Ruairi was most certainly a ten. I collected Ruairi in a taxi on the way into town but noticed something was off immediately.

'Are you alright? Have you been drinking?'

'Yeah, Paddy, I'll be honest. I've been drinking all day.' I was left with a choice: head in on my own, or bring drunken Ruairi with me. I just said, 'Fuck it,' and brought him. I knew he'd be a bit of craic at worst. We went to Chelsea's hotel and waited for her and her friend, Kayleigh, in the hotel lobby. The minute Kayleigh arrived, Ruairi stood up, three empty bottles on the table next to him, and shouted, 'You are fucking massive, love.' The poor girl didn't have a clue that in Dublin, 'massive' means you're good-looking.

'What? What do you mean by that?' Poor Ruairi couldn't comprehend why she was angry with him. We ended up going to a comedy show at the Laughter Lounge that evening but that was disastrous too. Ruairi just kept drinking and drinking, and then started heckling the comedian. I was mortified, trying to hide in my seat as Ruairi continued to shout, 'That's not funny, mate.' I made my mind up, he had to go.

'Please, Paddy, don't send me home. I'm having a great time.' I felt like an old fella trying to send my son back to bed and that definitely wasn't helping things with the girls. Eventually, they decided they were going to go one way and poor ol' drunken Ruairi and I were going to go another. I thought my chances were ruined and that I'd probably never see Chelsea again after that. I was furious and we headed to the Brewery Bar in Dublin 8, one of the dodgiest, run-down pubs in Dublin city centre.

'You fucked that for me, Ruairi.' But an hour later, my phone rang and it was Chelsea.

'Where are you? I'll come to meet you.'

I couldn't believe it, I was down but definitely not out. Chelsea and Kayleigh got into a taxi and headed for the Brewery Bar. When they pulled up outside, the taxi driver was insistent.

'I can't leave you out here, it's not safe.'

Eventually, he agreed that he'd wait outside until they came back out and gave him the signal that everything was okay. The old fellas in the bar nearly fell off their stools when this platinum blonde from Liverpool strolled into their local. We made up with Chelsea and Kayleigh, and ended up back in Lillie's Bordello. Chelsea and I were able to find a quiet corner for ourselves and just enjoy the night together. We kissed and danced the night away and I just knew it was going to be the start of something special. As the night came to an end, we went for a walk along the Liffey. Our own fairy-tale. I'm looking forward to telling my grandchildren how I met their grandmother.

Chelsea flew back to Liverpool the next morning and although we'd had a great time, I didn't know if she felt the same way I did. That uncertainty made me want her more. My ankle was still injured and I couldn't train, so I booked a trip over to Liverpool. Before long, Chelsea was showing me her side of the world as we walked hand-in-hand through Merseyside. Chelsea's family welcomed me into their home, which was in a council estate in Liverpool, showing me we had a lot more in common than I thought. I needed someone in my life who wasn't involved in my fighting and training. I needed affection, and affection that wasn't related to punching someone repeatedly in the head. Chelsea and I took turns flying over and back from Liverpool to Dublin and for the first time in as long as I could remember, an unfamiliar feeling consumed me, and it was one that I wanted to keep. I was beginning to feel true happiness.

The goodbyes were getting harder with each trip to the airport. One afternoon we decided to grab lunch before I flew back to Dublin. I was feeling adventurous so I decided to order a bowl of pea and ham soup. It was my way of showing Chelsea that I was interested in learning more about Merseyside and her life. However, the minute I got into my car in Dublin Airport, I was in bits. I was certain the British had planted a pea and ham soup bomb in my stomach and then waited until I was back in Ireland to detonate it. I knew it was food poisoning. I put the pedal down, driving over 100 miles per hour down the motorway, doing everything I could to make it home. I made it to the house just in time and launched myself into the bathroom.

John had a knack for ringing at the most awkward times, and this one was no different. When I saw his name, I knew it was a call I had to take, whether I was mid-date with the toilet bowl or not. A call from John was never to see if you were alright; it usually meant he had something to say.

'Vaughan Lee is coming over to the gym,' he told me. 'Do you want to spar him tomorrow?'

Lee was a fighter I could very easily have been matched against in my next bout, and he had already spoken about a drop to flyweight.

'Ah, John, he could be in my division. What's the story with him coming over?'

'You guys will never face each other. Sure it's good to see what level you're at.'

I had already sparred Neil Seery and Artemij Sitenkov's coach and now I was going to be sparring Lee. It was strange that John would allow these guys into the gym. There were enough people out there to spar. I didn't want someone in my division to get a read off me, be it a positive or negative one. If I gave Lee a hiding on that day, he probably wouldn't sign a contract to fight me. It made absolutely no sense to spar with him. When you're walking into a cage, it's the unknown that forces you to dig deep within yourself and find that inner strength. I didn't want to toy with that. That uncomfortable feeling was my fuel.

'Well, can you make it or not?' John asked.

'John, I'm in bits here.'

'Paddy, I need to know. Can you make it?'

'Alright, fuck it. I'll make it.'

I hung up the phone and went back to sitting on the toilet, leaning forward towards the sink. Pea and fucking ham soup.

The next day I turned up to the gym and met Vaughan Lee. I had spent the previous thirteen hours ridding myself of every bodily fluid I had, and felt completely drained. This was worse than any weight cut but I decided to go ahead with the sparring anyway. We started with MMA, then jiu-jitsu on the ground, and even practised some fence sparring. Lee was one of the top bantamweights in Europe so there was no doubt we were on a collision course. I felt the sparring went really well for me, and maybe he felt it went well for him too because a week or so later, the phone call from the UFC came to say we had been matched. There was a big card coming up in Glasgow and we were on it. It was a weird one — had Lee come over to see what I was like and then decided to fight me? I didn't know but I really didn't care. Although he likely had a read on me, there was an ace up my sleeve. I'd spent the thirteen hours prior to sparring sprawled out on the bathroom floor. Take the pea and ham soup out of the situation and I was a much more dangerous and confident opponent.

The Boston fight had been the last one on my original UFC contract but when we sat down, the discussions were fairly straightforward and I extended for a further four fights. My new contract put me in the highest-paid flyweights at the time and I was much happier. The pay was increasing to $17,000 to show and $17,000 to win for the first fight, so the step up was pretty steep considering I had started on $8,000 + $8,000.

The 50/50 model employed by the UFC can be the loneliest clause in a contract. If you've been knocked out, submitted, or even lost by a decision, it's not enough that you have to deal with the anger and disappointment of that crushing loss, but you also lose 50% of the money on the table. To make things worse, you then have to deal with clueless drunken fans stuffing their faces with burgers and hot dogs telling you how crap you are. That was the part of the game I despised most. People can't understand what a fighter goes through before even stepping into the cage unless they've been through it themselves. Unless you've stood in front of 14,000 people with everything on the line, it's very hard to understand the magnitude of that experience. Being in there is daunting, and you can have all the understanding and knowledge from training, but unless you do it on the most dangerous stage, you know nothing. For a promoter to withhold 50% of a fighter's pay when they were going through hell inside and outside the cage, it never sat well with me.

The UFC offered me a choice between Louis Smolka in Las Vegas or Vaughan Lee in Glasgow, and I went with Lee because it just made sense at that time travel-wise. We were expecting another Dublin card to be announced, so I knew I had to start making a name for myself on my own cards. An Irishman fighting an Englishman in Scotland, I knew the Glasgow crowd would be electric. Not having to fly to America made more sense to me too, as I didn't want to be away from Tiernan for so long. I was excited. There was no one else from SBG fighting on the card, and it was time for the Hooligan to get the spotlight. I understood fully that Conor was the superstar, the driving force not just for SBG but for Irish MMA as a whole, but John was now going to be hands-on with me and I'd have his undivided attention.

The excitement was short-lived, however, as the camp wasn't a good one. My ankle was still damaged from the Boston fight, but we kept that information within the team. I posted a picture on social media with the caption, 'Four weeks out and I'll do anything,' but the reality was that I had to lean on one ankle to keep the weight off the other just to take the photo. I was in big trouble. Running was difficult, grappling too. Swimming became my best friend. A physio, Dee Ryan, was working on me and she was a blessing, rehabbing my back and foot without charging me anything. I was looking after my weight cut, training and rehab as well as teaching three classes a week for John in the gym, and it was a lot for me to tackle on my own. John wouldn't take a cut from my purse but I'd worked countless hours for him every single week for almost ten years teaching and promoting the gym. There's a perception that John came in and trained us for nothing until we all hit the big time. It might have been different for other people, but that wasn't the case for me.

Fighting in Glasgow gave me another opportunity to fly Tiernan out to watch me again so Adam and his girlfriend, Sam, brought him over. Things were getting more serious between me and Chelsea, and I had introduced her to Tiernan on one of her visits to Dublin. I felt it was important that Denise knew who her son was meeting, and when I told her about Chelsea, she wished me well. The next day, she phoned me and said she was also seeing someone else: the guy she worked with.

'So the lad that's been in your phone for all of these years, this is now the lad you're seeing?'

She had promised me months earlier that I would be mad to think it was him.

'Yeah, but we didn't start seeing each other until I was single, Paddy. He asked me out.'

I was no fool. Tiernan had told me that Denise had been taking him out to meet a man of his description, even when we were still together. Our relationship changed from that day forward.

The week building up to the Glasgow fight was a nice one. I had Team Midget with me and we walked around the city, getting in sessions every day. My emotions were running high, but in a positive sense, and I was proud of how far I had come.

Here in the madness of the UFC, the bright lights and sharp rights, I still felt like I was the same old Paddy Holohan from the council estate in Jobstown. Nothing had changed for me. My mate Macker sent me a picture of the road that week with the caption 'This is where it all began, remember.' How could I forget? That road forged me.

The weight cut that week was okay but I still hated every minute of it. While everyone went down for dinner, I stayed in the hotel room cooking chicken fillets on my George Foreman. One scary moment will always remain with me. As I tried to cut the final few pounds, the team stripped me naked and laid me out on the hotel room floor. When I tried to sit up, the entire room went black. I couldn't see a thing, as if my eyes had given up on me. I didn't know what was really going on, but I didn't really give a fuck either. Was I now blind? I didn't care about the effect it would have on my life; I just wanted to be ready for the fight. I knew years of cutting weight was taking its toll on my body, and now it appeared my eyes had had enough too. Here I was, stark naked in front of a room of people and everything had gone dark. I kept thinking about the fight and nothing else. Was I even in any fit state to fight? But then, just as quickly as it had gone, my sight returned. I'd love to say that I took stock of the moment and the dangers that I was putting my body through, but I didn't. I didn't give a fuck, I just wanted to make weight and get on that stage.

I was finally on weight leaving the hotel but when I arrived, somehow I was one pound over. I had done absolutely everything but it still wasn't enough. I was angry and frustrated, but there was no point in wasting time. I threw on a sauna suit and began running up and down the back stairs. My body was dry and I was finding it hard to sweat. I was barely conscious at times, but that last pound was my final hurdle.

I could tell that Lee was having a tough cut too so I used that to my advantage.

'Losing a few pounds there, Vaughan?' I laughed at him.

He was struggling, and it was the first time that I had ever seen anyone break in front of me on the scales. I weighed in on target and made my way to the centre of the stage for the staredown. I always found the staredown such an important part of the battle, and I loved the fact that I could smell my opponent. I tried to sniff as much of him as I could. My primal instincts took over. In those moments, it's like putting two Rottweilers head to head, each one ready to chew the other's face off. I've never been shy in those moments and I've never forced a way of behaving or an act. It all comes naturally to me.

The staredown is the first slow-motion jab in a frenetic bloodbath. I stood over Lee and looked straight into his eyes, and I could tell he didn't want this victory as badly as I needed it. I could feel a scowl on my face but I wasn't angry. I was looking straight through him, focused. He stepped forward, took off his glasses and smiled at me. It set off a trigger in my head. If I had a dagger I would have stabbed him on the stage in that moment and barely blinked. As he stepped forward, I leaned into him, staring deeper into his eyes, but there was nothing there. Just emptiness. His whole body deflated, punctured by his fear and my resolve. It was as if the reality of the situation had finally hit home for him. If he wanted the victory, he would have to spark me out cold.

'Whoa, someone won that weigh-in anyway,' John said to me as I walked off the stage. Vaughan Lee was in trouble.

On the day of the fight, I woke up and brought Tiernan to a local carnival. I was beginning to get noticed by the Glaswegians, but they were respectful and allowed me to just get on with my day. I even went on the waltzers, which probably wasn't the brightest idea on the morning of a UFC fight, but I would do anything to make Tiernan happy. As the fight got nearer, the same old ritual started to take shape. The only difference was that Chelsea would be there and I wanted to share with her the madness of it all.

'Five minutes and the bus will be downstairs.'

Three o'clock arrived and we headed over to the arena. Trying to find a cup of tea when you're fighting outside of Ireland is always a nightmare and it took me forever to find one in Glasgow before the fight. I eventually did but it was nothing like the tea I was used to in Ireland. I went upstairs to the dressing room for a nap, something that had become a part of my preparation, a ritual I tried to include ever since I was told in France that 'the dangerous ones sleep'. I forced myself to fall asleep, even just for a short period, in order to reset my mind. The first time I did it, I wanted to test my own strength of mind and see if I could fully relax during the anxiety and madness of fight day, and to my surprise, I could. I remember asking myself, does that mean I'm dangerous? Wrapped in the Ireland flag, I fell asleep in the corner and before I knew it, John woke me. It was time.

The adrenalin kicked in. John set up rounds and got me moving in certain ways with a purpose to everything. His presence was felt immediately. He had Ais sparring with me for the first round, Richie Smullen the next. This was exactly what I needed for the fight. The dressing room isn't where fights are won, but it's certainly where a lot of them are lost. It's a delicate place and I needed someone to listen to me, to keep me calm, and to answer the silly questions I blurt out before a fight. John is world class at that aspect of the dressing room, and it showed that night in Glasgow.

When the call came and it was time for the walk, I had the flag in my hand and waited for my music, 'Celtic Symphony' by the Wolfe Tones, to drop, knowing that it would cause mayhem in the arena. I remember someone saying to me afterwards that I was braver walking out to that song in Glasgow than I was getting into the cage to fight. The division between the Catholic and Protestant sides of the city was not something to mess with. That song set the crowd on fire and I revelled in the madness. The music blasted through the speakers and was immediately met with a chorus of boos on one side, and a wave of elation from the other. It had the perfect reaction, splitting the crowd. Us versus them, just how I planned it. Vaughan Lee was about to face a version of Paddy Holohan unlike any he had experienced before. He may have had black belts but I had a Jobstown passport, and I know which one I'd prefer in a dogfight.

I can usually remember every aspect of my fights but this one was different. I was so focused that it was almost like an out-of-body experience. On one occasion, I caught Lee in a triangle and felt like I was about to finish him, but then he caught me with a punch right into the eye. A quick smack, and I could feel the swelling setting in immediately. There were little pockets of these moments throughout the fight, where I felt in total control but then he would surprise me with a counter or clean strike. He was there for the taking but remained dangerous throughout. He took my back at one stage and locked in a choke, but I got out of it. Next, he mounted me but I had been working on a lot of leg locks with Richie Smullen in the build-up to the fight, and somehow was able to escape. I threw my legs over, rolled him off, and got into the heel hook position. I could barely believe it myself but now I was in a strong position to finish him. I pulled on the heel hook but he somehow rolled out and the chance was gone. If I had gotten that opportunity later in my career, I've no doubt I would have finished him there and then. That's something I love about MMA; the older you get, the better you become.

I dominated Lee throughout with the exception of one or two tricky moments, and as the clock wound down, I knew the fight was over. I had gotten the better of him on the mat but also with a lot of the stand-up. He was there for the taking so I decided I'd try to get the finish. I shot for the takedown, landed some shots in the guard, but he stayed strong. The bell rang but there was only one outcome: a unanimous decision victory, and I moved to 3-1 in the UFC.

Vaughan Lee was a tough opponent, a veteran of the game, and it filled me with great satisfaction to leave Glasgow with a victory over someone as respected as he was. I had earned John's approval and it made me feel great. I finally felt like I was a proper founding member of SBG in the eyes of the person who mattered most to me in MMA. To be able to make some noise and garner attention in a camp that Conor McGregor was involved in was an incredible achievement personally, too, because it proved to people that I wasn't just piggy-backing on Conor's limelight. And that was a mantra that Conor pushed himself a lot. He was the ultimate teammate, always putting the emphasis on 'us' as opposed to just him. The Irish invasion, us against them, one of us goes to war, we all go to war. Conor always cared about the collective and not just the individual. He was a proper leader. The words he used were always 'us', 'our' and 'we', never 'I' or 'me'.

There was a world of difference between a 2-2 record and a 3-1 record and the significance of that wasn't lost on me. I knew how important victory over Lee was. Getting a title shot was a huge goal of mine, and it was edging closer and closer. I was now on a two-fight win streak and knew that one more would put me in the conversation for a fight against Demetrious Johnson, the champion. I knew what I had to do: fight Louis Smolka, beat him, and then call out 'Mighty Mouse'. I stepped forward to the microphone and faced the crowd.

'There's a guy that got a win against one of us Irish guys, put him in here against me.' I called Louis Smolka out, and by the time I stepped out of the cage, word had already come through that Smolka said 'challenge accepted' in principle. It was on.

I caught a flight back to Dublin with Tiernan and when we touched down on the runway, an announcement came over the PA system.

'We'd just like to thank Paddy Holohan and his son, and congratulate him on his win last night.'

Tiernan went mental. 'Oh my God, Dad! They've just said your name. That's so cool!'

I got a round of applause from everyone on the plane and it felt amazing. I had two UFC cheques in my bags, my son on my left side, and a wonderful girlfriend. I just didn't need anything else in my life. I was right where I needed to be.

Paddy Holohan, 12-1 — July 2015

CHAPTER 13 ....

'If you put €80,000 into the building, we can have a conversation,' John said to the two local lads who approached him about setting up a gym in Tallaght.

'Forget them, Paddy,' he told me afterwards. 'We're going to open our own gym.'

It turned out to be the first step in a long journey that would see the two of us open a gym together. I don't know if John was fully aware of how much I looked up to him, but he certainly knew how much I cared about him. He was my father figure and SBG was my family. That was programmed into my DNA. I was missing that link my entire life, and once I found MMA, it changed everything. I knew that if I could create that feeling for someone else, especially in my own community, then it could have the same effect on them. That was why I wanted to set up a gym.

It all happened pretty quickly, I was sparring in the gym before the Vaughan Lee fight and John approached me with the idea of going into business together.

'Forty thousand each, Paddy. We can set it up in Tallaght. You can run the gym and Chelsea can be the manager. I'll even train her in for six months in SBG Concorde first.'

I was both excited and nervous, but it seemed like the perfect opportunity for me to give back to my community, particularly with John by my side. I would have followed John into a burning building that day if he had asked. I had a strong relationship with his parents, his sister, his nephews, his nieces. We were all so tight and he was more than just my coach. I immediately accepted the offer, we shook hands, and hugged across the table, toasting to the next chapter. Owning a gym in Tallaght had been a dream of mine since the day I fell in love with MMA.

It was a big moment, the beginning of my transition from MMA fighter to business owner. I had put about €60,000 aside for a plan like this and it was an opportunity that I could not let pass. John and I met with solicitors and began the steps of drafting contracts and setting up bank accounts. Conor was spending much more time in Vegas, so John was flying over and back with him, meaning it was on me to find a building in Tallaght for our gym. I spent the guts of a year looking at various buildings around the area, but it became increasingly difficult to find the right place. We were beginning to worry that maybe we'd never find the right spot, but that all changed one evening on the mats.

'Paddy, you won't believe what's after happening,' John said. 'A silent investor has offered to pay for the whole gym. We'll never see him and both of us will just have to operate the gym. We won't even have to put our €40,000 in. The guy is going to put the money in, and we'll build a team and have a meeting next week to iron out the finer details.'

I was excited, but apprehensive. The deal sounded too good to be true, but I trusted John and it sounded like a great opportunity. The following week we met with the investor, but the minute I walked in the door, every instinct I had carved from my upbringing told me this was a bad idea. I knew straight away that getting into business with this guy was going to be a major mistake. The only thing he kept referring to was 'Conor McGregor', which made me think he was using us in order to get nearer to Conor. He proceeded to tell us the same story that we would hear time and again over the next few months: that his wife was close to the King of Malaysia, that he was very wealthy, and that he was going to change the game. He continuously referred to himself as the 'silent investor', but I'm not sure he knew what that meant given his propensity to put himself front and centre.

The talks progressed and even though I still had my reservations, we reached what sounded like a good deal in principle: the investor would pay for the gym, Chelsea would be the manager, I'd be in charge, and John would focus on SBG Concorde. It didn't take long before I started to notice cracks appearing, and when it came to the issue of ownership, I was being treated as an employee rather than a partner.

'You'll get €2,000 per month in wages, Paddy.'

I immediately questioned John on this.

'Wages? I'm not going to be putting my face and name on a building in Tallaght for a measly wage. It's my reputation and they're my people. It won't be John Kavanagh's gym to the people of Tallaght, it will be mine. If something goes wrong in that building, it's my door they'll be knocking on. I have to own a part of this gym or else I'm not getting involved.'

'Okay, Paddy, we'll tie up all those bits later, but for now, is everyone happy to proceed?' We shook hands and did our best to move forward.

I had spent a huge amount of time trying to get the gym off the ground when nobody else would or could, and now it felt like I was being pushed out. The gym needed a coach and a face, and I made it clear that if I was going to be running the place and taking all the responsibility, I wouldn't be doing it for €2,000 a month. If I was going to be on a salary, I told them that I wanted a percentage stake in what we were building as well. In a meeting in McDonald's on the Long Mile Road, we came to an agreement.

My star was rising massively off the back of two strong wins over Shane Howell and Vaughan Lee, and I knew the UFC was coming back to Dublin. I was fully sure I would be fighting Louis Smolka on the card, both because of the show I had put on the last time, and also because he had agreed in principle to fight me. Even when people asked me if I was fighting on the card, I would answer by saying, 'Yeah, I'm the main event.' I'm a strong believer in the law of attraction and that event was made for me.

When the call finally came and I found out that I wasn't main event for UFC Fight Night 76 in Dublin, I was angry. I deserved that main event but they were giving it to Joseph Duffy. Joe hadn't earned it, and the UFC were giving him that spot to build him up ahead of a potential fight with Conor. He hadn't even fought in Ireland for a long time. I was a hometown hero, and the UFC was on my doorstep. I could get the Luas door to door, and my housing estate had a direct line to the arena. Joe's didn't. My relationship with Joe's name was a strange one too; I always took exception to him allowing himself to be called 'Irish Joe', which I felt was derogatory and disrespectful. If someone called me Irish Joe on a building site, I would have hit them with a shovel.

It was a quick turnaround and was going to be my fifth UFC fight in fifteen months. Nobody was fighting at that pace. To me, I was there to fight everybody and get to the top of the ladder as soon as possible. I didn't see how drained I was, but coming up to the fight, I was exhausted mentally. Within twelve months, I had cut 20lb per fight to make weight, a total of 80lb on and off in the space of a year. The mental and physical aspect of that was certainly taking its toll on my body, and that was before taking into account any of the fighting. I thought back to what Firas Zahabi had said to me after my loss in Canada. Back then, I couldn't understand why he was encouraging me to slow down and take a break. In my mind, I just fought as often as I could.

Chelsea and I were madly in love but all the travel back and forth was taking its toll on us, particularly while I was in camp, so she decided to move over three weeks before the Dublin card. It was a huge move for her, to leave her family and move country, but we knew we had something special and she made the sacrifice for the good of our relationship, something I was eternally grateful for. We probably should have waited until after the fight for Chelsea to move over, as the move wasn't as straightforward as we had hoped; it definitely added more stress to an already stressful camp. After five days, Chelsea even said, 'That's it, I'm going home, I'm going home,' but luckily she changed her mind. We still laugh about that today.

The preparation for that card wasn't what I had come to expect after the highs of the Vaughan Lee fight. My back was creaking again and causing me pain. Some days I wanted to train but I simply couldn't, and had to sit by the sidelines and watch. Running had always made me feel good mentally as well as physically, but I couldn't even do that. Tactically, there was very little structure, and even less of a game plan. There was no discussion around how I could pick Louis Smolka apart, nor were there any tailored sessions focusing on his areas of weakness. I needed a lot more one-on-one time with my coach, but the situation with the gym was affecting my relationship with John. I felt that I had paid my dues and that it was my time to be given the attention I needed in training, but John appeared uninterested.

I stayed at home on fight week as I thought it would be a lot more comfortable, but it was a mistake and I should have stayed in the fighters' hotel. Instead, I gave the hotel to Sunna from Mjolnir to repay her for giving me the room in Iceland, so that she could bring her daughter to stay in Dublin that week. I should have stuck with the usual routine and stayed in the hotel. At home, I just couldn't fall into the same battlefield mindset. If I was around the hotel, I would have seen Smolka a bit more, which always gives an added edge. There's no animosity between myself and my opponent, and I know that they're just trying to get the most out of their life too, but seeing them definitely forces you to hone in on the task at hand.

I had come to peace with the notion that I was an entertainer and that the people in the crowd were the crazy ones, the addicts. They were the ones paying money to see a man succeed or fail. One person is at the high point of their life while the other is hitting rock bottom, and the crowd pay money to watch it. If people think we're crazy for getting in a ring and fighting for money, then they're definitely crazier if they're willing to pay to watch it. It's like the gladiators back in Roman times. Very often it was the people in the seats of the Colosseum who were the most barbaric. When I'm in the cage, I'm the normal one. I have a reason to be in there. What's yours?

The week before the fight, the card took a major hit when Stipe Miocic got injured and had to withdraw from his co-main event fight with Ben Rothwell. Norman Parke's fight against Reza Madadi was elevated to co-main event, and that hurt me. I should have been given that chance above anyone else on the card, particularly when I was coming off the back of two strong victories. That morning, Chelsea woke me with good news. She had been on Twitter and seen the news that my fight had been pushed up to co-main event instead. I didn't really care if I was the first or last fight. I just wished someone had had the decency to phone me rather than finding out through a tweet.

The week of the fight, Chelsea was incredible. Although she was homesick, she put everything to one side to make sure I had everything I needed. She prepared all my food, my gear, organised my logistics and media commitments. It allowed me to focus on making weight. I was carb depleted for an entire week, sticking to the chicken and nut butter, and that's always tough. These days, fighters work with some of the best nutritionists available but back then, Chelsea was my chef and that worked for me. Whatever problems we encountered, we solved them as best we could. As Theodore Roosevelt said, 'The credit belongs to the man who is actually in the arena, whose face is marred by dust and sweat and blood; who strives valiantly; who errs, who comes short again and again, because there is no effort without error and shortcoming.'

The day before the weigh-in, I was lying in bed again and Chelsea woke me with more good news

'Paddy, you're not going to believe this. You're the main event!'

'What? How do you know? You just woke up.'

It was all over Twitter. Joseph Duffy had a concussion and was off the card. I liked Joe but this situation really made me angry. He had received a strike to the head during training that week and when the UFC sent him for medical tests, the doctors found that he had suffered a mild concussion and ruled him out of the fight. It put the entire event in jeopardy. I could not believe that he would risk a heavy shot to the head in training just three days out from the fight, and the fact that I only ended up as the main event because of his negligence pissed me off even more. If I had been the main event from the start, it would have changed everything for me, financially, mentally, and even in terms of my own legacy, but now that my opportunity had arrived, it felt somewhat tainted. I was given two days' notice that I was the main event fighter, and there was no communication of an increase in pay and a massive increase in my media obligations at a critical period in fight week. The worst thing about it was that the entire event had been sold out but when Joe was ruled out, people started returning their tickets. My whole housing estate wanted to go and were screaming for tickets from the start so when tickets became available again, the event sold out again immediately on the back of my support. The whole situation angered me at a time when I needed to keep a cool head. Becoming main event didn't change much for Louis Smolka; everything rested on my shoulders. I gave an interview on national TV in Ireland.

'Give back the tickets,' I told people. 'Give them all back if you want, but make sure you put an advertisement on in Jobstown, 'cause my whole housing estate would fill this arena alone.'

I took everything in my stride as best I could and just kept pushing forward towards fight night. I stood backstage at the weigh-ins, tricolour in my hand, ready to make the walk.

Aisling was on the card too, and so were Paul Redmond and Neil Seery. Seery had fought Smolka a few months earlier and lost by unanimous decision, and I probably should have leaned on him a bit more for advice. But I was tired. As much as I tried, I just couldn't shake off the lethargy. I was exhausted and just wanted the fight to come around.

Smolka walked out first for the weigh-ins and I could hear the reaction from backstage. It was a respectful one and there was barely any booing, but when I emerged from the shadows, the place went wild. I embraced every second of it, every shriek, every shout, and not only that, I could recognise the faces in the crowd. These were people I had met throughout my journey, these were my people. All the anger and uncertainty I had been feeling was gone. I didn't give a fuck anymore. I was floating. I was now standing in the position where I had watched Conor tell Diego Brandao that he was going to take his head clean off, and as cool as that was, I knew I would have to deliver a line to the crowd to send them wild again. I weighed in and stared at Smolka but could immediately see that he was just like me; one of the kids who wouldn't give up. I could see the toughness in him but it only excited me further. This was going to be a hell of a knock. I turned around to the crowd and said, 'It's us against them.' That sent the Irish crowd wild. It wasn't as strong as 'We're not here to take part, we're here to take over,' but it served its purpose.

It had been a long day and we had been hanging around for ages, so I was in a rush to get home. I just wanted to clear my head, get into my own bed and prepare for the fight. It was time for me to start focusing on Louis Smolka because the madness of the week meant that I didn't have a huge amount of time to do so. On our way back to Tallaght, Chelsea took a wrong turn and ended up adding almost two hours to a thirty-minute journey because of the Friday rush hour traffic in Dublin. I wasn't the most pleasant person to be around at that time anyway, but now here we were sitting in traffic with no chance of moving for a couple of hours. By the time we got home that night it was 8pm and I still needed to eat. It wasn't Chelsea's fault, I had fucked up my own preparation completely and should have just stayed in the hotel. This entire fight would eventually come down to small steps and I was already taking the wrong ones.

I woke the next day in my own bed in Jobstown, just like I had done thousands of times, but that day was different. It was the morning of the biggest fight of my career. I slept so well, but woke early, ready for war. I always woke up alert on the morning of a fight, as if a switch went off and I was ready to leap out from under the covers. I was never nervous, not at that stage. Losing was not something that scared me, and neither was dying. If it happened, I would deal with it. I understood the dangers and had come to terms with that. Chelsea was out running errands and I was in the house on my own, so I grabbed the dog and went out for a walk. The minute I left the house, I could see people were staring at me thinking, 'What is this lunatic doing walking his dog the morning of the biggest fight of his life?'

'Paddy, are you still fighting tonight?'

'Ah yeah, of course,' and I just kept on walking. I had walked these footpaths so many times during my life, but now here I was, still the same Paddy Holohan strolling through Jobstown with a smile on my face, but about to be the main event on a UFC card in my hometown. No matter what happened that night, I'd remember that moment for ever.

As I was the main event, my fight the last one on the card and much later than I had been used to. The last time I fought in Dublin, I was sitting in my seat having won by half past five, but that wouldn't be the case on this particular night. Being main event brings a lot of added pressure, but there are other differences too, like dealing with an empty dressing room where loneliness can set in. I was used to busy dressing rooms but I knew as the last one out, I'd be the only fighter in my dressing room. I had experienced that before in my fights in small arenas and tried to brace myself for it, but this time was different. This was the main event of a UFC show and it felt different right from the moment I pulled up to the arena. Upon my arrival, I was greeted with posters everywhere, saying 'Holohan vs Smolka'. It was like a dream. I remember seeing Conor's face on bins in Boston and now here I was, my face plastered all over Dublin, and for all the right reasons. Regardless of the outcome, I was going to become only the second Irishman in the history of the UFC to have my own main event.

I entered the dressing room and Ais was there warming up for her fight. She had been fighting a lot in a short period of time, and the weight cuts affected her too. I felt like I had acquired a borderline eating disorder from all the mental and physical pain I had put my body through from cutting weight, and I had no doubt others were dealing with the same internal struggles. I walked in, gave her a hug and could see she was fully in the zone. She took control of the entire room herself and it made me proud to see her finally doing things her own way. Ais and I were close for so long and she was a good friend. We had been through a lot and now here we were, at a milestone in our careers.

I found a corner of the dressing room and tried to set into my usual routine of falling asleep, making me believe I was a psychopath, but this time I just couldn't do it. It just wasn't clicking. At one point, I stood there looking out the window thinking, 'I'm just not firing today.' I didn't feel motivated, or excited, I was just flat. The spark was missing. I tried to suppress those thoughts as best I could but it was no use. I was in dangerous territory mentally.

The other fights on the card went well for my teammates and finally the time came to warm up, a moment that I have looked back on and dissected thousands of times for hours and hours. I started shadow-boxing and working on my movement, but there was no help from John. He was in the dressing room but he was on his phone the whole time. John ran my corner in Glasgow and it could not have gone better, but this was shaping up to be the opposite. Tommy Martin, Blaine O'Driscoll and Richie Smullen were in the dressing room with us, but John kept saying, 'Wait, wait, wait.' I ran one round with Tommy and started to feel a little better, but when Tommy asked if he should do another, John replied with a stern no, walking in and out of the dressing room on his phone. This was not the right atmosphere.

'He's not here with me today,' I thought. I should have stood up to John and told him to focus on the fight prep, but I didn't. I never stood up to John. The time to make the walk was approaching, and even Tommy and Richie were staring at me and pointing at John, unsure of what to do themselves.

'John, will I do another round?'

'No, no. Take your time.'

The five-minute call arrived and John jumped up, put his hands on my arm and said, 'Ah sure, you're warm anyway.' I was warm, but I wasn't fully warm in the way I should have been. If this was football, my body would have been warm but my touch wasn't ready. It was time to leave the dressing room and my mind was distracted. Fuck it, I thought, let's just get on with it and get him finished quickly. But that was the wrong way to think, I was taking Louis Smolka's resilience for granted.

As I made the walk to the cage, the security took us the wrong way and down through the bar. People were everywhere, all screaming my name, and as good as that felt, it probably wasn't the best route to take prior to such a massive fight. We arrived at the entrance and waited for the countdown to the entrance music, a sacred moment in any fighter's preparation. But instead of being able to concentrate and soak up that last moment of tranquillity, John, who was usually calm, was back on his phone again, arguing with a UFC official this time. In the week leading up to the fight, John had arranged tickets for a young kid named Carlos. Carlos had passed his Junior Certificate exams while he was homeless, which was an incredible achievement, and John and the UFC made the lovely gesture of congratulating him by bringing him down to the gym to meet the fighters that week and giving him tickets to fight night. But when he showed up that night, he was refused entry, and now John was in the middle of full-blown argument, seconds before the TV cameras were due to be pointed at my face for the most important walk of my life.

'Hang up the fucking phone, John.'

He put the phone away, but Louis Smolka was the last thing on my mind. John said afterwards that the entire event overwhelmed me, but those who were present in the dressing room know that wasn't the case. I loved every fucking bit of it. Every pair of eyes, every scream, the smell of the alcohol in the air. It was life-giving. There was no way any fight overwhelmed me. Fighting was all I knew and I had been doing it my entire life.

As I made the walk to the cage, I just didn't give a fuck any more. I wanted to put it all behind me and get on with the task at hand. I walked out to 'Paint the Town Green' by The Script, but it didn't give me the same boost that 'Celtic Symphony' or 'Ten Thousand Hours' or 'Salvation' gave me. The place was jam-packed to the rafters, and my son was sitting in the front row. No matter what happened over the next three rounds, seeing his father walk in as the main event at a UFC fight is something nobody will ever be able to take away from him. Conor was in the front row too and he gave me a wink and a thumbs up, that 'Well done, you've made it' seal of approval. Just a year and a half earlier, I was sitting in the arena watching him fight as the main event, and now here I was. I tried to take in as much as I could because I didn't know if I would ever get the chance to do something like that again. I walked up the steps, threw my hands in the air to the crowd and said, 'Fuck it, let's do this.'

As soon as we touched gloves, I started strongly, right from the first exchange. We hit into a clinch and ended up against the cage, and I was able to take Smolka down with ease. I was able to put a kimura arm lock on him, which took me by surprise. This was easy. In that moment, I nearly won the fight and remember thinking, 'It's not going to be this easy, is it?' Maybe in that thirty seconds, the aura of the entire occasion had gotten to him. It took serious cojones to walk into an arena full of screaming Irish fans and try to take down their hometown hero. I tried to rip his arm off with the kimura, but Louis stood up and got out of it.

I had let my first chance slip by, but I soon got another one, and that was the moment that the entire fight would ultimately hinge on. I took Smolka's back and had one hand on his neck but he was able to trap my other one. Although I was able to get a body triangle on, I made a huge mistake in the fact that I wasn't relaxed enough. I was trying to force everything. I couldn't hear John. The only person I could hear was Conor, who was screaming advice at me from cageside. I had Smolka's back and was in a position where I'd finished people thousands of times on the mats and throughout my career, but this one felt different. I had one hand around him and he still had my other one trapped.

'Just finish this, Paddy. This is the one,' I told myself. 'If you finish this choke, you win.'

It was so close. I pulled my hand but he spun into me and I ended up on the bottom, in guard again. That deflated me. I should have been prepared for the disappointment of not finishing a good submission opportunity and just allowed the moment to pass, but I couldn't get it out of my head. Smolka's superpower was his ability to to go all the way into deep submissions and survive, and I had just experienced it first-hand. This wasn't going to be as straightforward as I had thought. He spun back into me and we ended up in guard, but then the bell rang and we went back to our corners. I had won the round, but I had let a good opportunity pass without fully capitalising on it.

The second round was much closer than the first with a lot of back and forth between us. Smolka was getting stronger, growing into the fight, and then it happened. Towards the end of the round, he caught me clean and I was so tired that I just couldn't close my hands any more. There were fifty-one seconds left in the round when I got caught. I had been in control, but now I was no longer tired. I was exhausted. Worst of all, I was aware of that exhaustion and that's a dangerous feeling. I should have started to move around the cage, buying myself time, but my instinct forced me to do the opposite. I kept moving forward and before I knew it, my body was in the danger zone of non-recovery, and I was in deep trouble. Smolka could sense I was struggling and started to apply more and more strikes. I made a huge error after that, deciding to fight back and shoot for a takedown. I regretted it instantly, throwing myself into a vulnerable position that he capitalised on. He mounted me and started to unleash more shots, so I had no choice but to show my back. Just as I turned, I felt his hand grab my throat and it was deep immediately. I was in big trouble. He timed it well and his execution was outstanding. I had been in that position before, but this time it was different. I was exhausted, physically and mentally. The outcome seemed inevitable.

It's such a strange thing, the human body. Mine was in survival mode and ordinarily would try everything it could to fight against that choke, but not this time. This was the day I would truly surrender in that cage. It was like my body had enough of the torture I was putting it through and it was time to accept it. Moments like that have a long-term effect on a person. Smolka had brought me right to the edge of the cliff, and my body was ready to just jump off. I died in my head. This was different from a knockout or a strike to the head. I was being strangled in front of thousands of people, my windpipe was being crushed with no way to escape, and my reaction was just to embrace it. Death was always a huge part of my life, knocking at my door but running away by the time I answered. This time felt different, though. This time, it was right there waiting for me.

I eventually tapped but it's not something I remember. In that moment, my mind chose to think about other things: Tiernan, Chelsea, my life. I've watched the video back and I remember the Hooligan saying to me, 'We're not fucking tapping. We're not.' I didn't want to tap, I didn't want to go out that way, but in that last moment, as the world started to turn black, it was the thought of Tiernan and my responsibility to him that made me tap. In hindsight, who really gives a fuck that I tapped, though? That's my loss, no one else's. I carry that. If tapping meant that Tiernan wouldn't have to witness his father choked unconscious in the cage in front of him, then I'd tap all day. I never realised that emotion was within me, but I always learned the most about myself from the lowest of lows. Winning that fight was the most important thing in my life just before I entered that cage. Two rounds later, all I cared about was my son. That might seem like a contradiction considering that I was risking my life every single time I fought, but I fought for the right reasons: for my son, for my family, and for my mental well-being. I don't know why I chose to tap in that moment but I do know it was the right decision. Would I risk my life and enter that cage again? Of course I fucking would.

The immediate aftermath of the fight was a strange experience. The entire crowd was on its feet baying for blood, screaming my name, but then I blacked out for a second and when I came to, the place was eerily silent. It's crazy how quickly these moments occur, two or three seconds that stay with you for the rest of your life. I could hear Smolka's footsteps, running off to his corner to celebrate, and I knew I had let my people down. The only voice I could hear was his distinctive Hawaiian brogue.

It's easy to win. You can celebrate and cheer and enjoy the fruits of your labour, but you learn a lot more about a person in defeat, and that's one thing that myself and my SBG teammates have always made sure to respect. There are millions of ways to win, but only one way to lose and that's to do it respectfully. There's no time for excuses. Take the loss and respect your opponent's win. Tiernan was watching me, and that's how I wanted him to see me behave. I caught his eye, gave him a little fist bump to reassure him that I was okay, and did the same to Conor. I could see the disappointment in their eyes but I did my best to keep the emotion inside. There would be plenty of time to be upset over the coming weeks and months.

When I got to the microphone, Dan Hardy, who had spoken to me during the highest highs of my career, asked me how I was feeling. It was the sorest, rawest, most emotional moment of my life, with 9,000 people there and a microphone in my face just after I had been nearly choked unconscious, but the words flowed without thought.

'I don't come out here and say that I'm talented or that I'm gifted, but I'll tell you one thing, when I come out here, I'll give you everything and that's it.'

The whole arena went from silence to an eruption of applause. Like a defibrillator, it shocked me back to life. I always knew that my fans were incredible. It didn't matter if I fell, they would always catch me and pick me up again. Win, lose, or draw, I was invincible. My people stood by me, even in defeat.

Not only had I lost, but I also had to be drug-tested. I wasn't worried but it was definitely frustrating because all I wanted was to curl up into a ball. I went upstairs to the medical area and John and Chelsea were waiting at the door. John put his hands out in front of him and gave a gentle shrug of his shoulders, as if to say these things happen.

'Don't worry about the loss,' he said. 'It is what it is, we'll go again.'

He handed me my stuff and I didn't see him again for a couple of weeks. No calls, no texts. It was clear he wasn't devastated. I was. It felt like the entire world was ashamed of me. I was a loser. Going outside the door and seeing people was excruciating, but instead of hiding away, I took it in my stride. Even the next day, I threw on my tracksuit and marched proudly through Jobstown.

'Too much, too soon' was how John described my reaction to being elevated to main event. He said that a seed of doubt had manifested and spread throughout my body, leading to my underperformance, but that wasn't fully true. To me, that analysis showed John's inability to share responsibility. My preparation was upset that night. The dressing room felt terrible and that set the tone for what happened next, not any sense of being overwhelmed or any self-doubt in my mind. I never blame anyone for any loss in my career. That falls on me. I take every loss, especially the Louis Smolka one, on the chin, and I have to live with it every single day. I sleep with it and still think about it in bed at night when nobody else does, not even Louis. If I had won that fight, a title shot was within my grasp, that was the reality. I was nearly at the top of the ladder and I needed someone to help push me up another rung, not someone who was distracted and would allow me to fall.

I was able to control my emotions while I was in the arena, but when I got back to the hotel room, I threw my head into the pillow and burst into tears. The reality of what had occurred had begun to sink in. They say you should always take note of who is there for you when you lose, not when you win, and Chelsea was the one who was by my side. I don't know what I would have done without her. If she wasn't there, I would have been in that hotel room by myself and anything could have happened. When you live your life at the pace I do, the highs are sky-high and the lows are unimaginably low. Chelsea doesn't realise it but she probably saved my life that night.

She told me that locking myself away in a hotel room was the wrong way to deal with the loss, and she was right. There was an afterparty booked for me in Dublin and although I didn't want to go, the fact that I had no 50% win bonus and the club was willing to pay me €3,000 meant that I had no real choice. As soon as I got there, I regretted it. Kiefer Crosbie, James Gallagher, my childhood friend Sean Roddy, and a few others were there to support me and I appreciated that, but I just didn't want to be there. Macker and Dean, two of my closest friends, they understood I was hurting and they took me to the side away from it all. I said a few words into the microphone, thanked people for coming, and then slipped out the side door. I went back to the hotel room and bawled my eyes out again.

Paddy Holohan, 12-2 — October 2015

CHAPTER 14 ....

The disappointment of losing in my own backyard took a long time to fade. I tried to switch my focus to working on the Tallaght gym in the hope that it would bring back some semblance of positivity. The UFC made sure I was looked after for the Dublin fight too, paying me the main event purse even though that was never discussed beforehand. I was expecting €15,000 but was delighted when a cheque for €60,000 arrived. It wasn't life-changing money but it definitely helped. I didn't buy anything crazy, and I even kept my banged-up Volvo so people wouldn't know that I had a few quid. It just wasn't in me to flash it. I began to pour my heart and soul into the Tallaght project, but the whole experience continued to throw up serious problems and the environment around it was toxic.

I took a couple of weeks out after the Smolka fight before getting back to training. I was expecting to be on a card in Rotterdam in May 2016 and that was my focus. I was still struggling with injury and tried to rest my back as best I could, but it was no use and the pain just wouldn't go away. I felt like I was back where I had been before I had the surgery.

In the UFC, if you get hurt while fighting, you're supposed to disclose your injuries and this time, I decided to follow the official protocol, a move that would prove to be fatal for my career as a professional mixed martial artist. I filed a report stating that my back and knee were causing serious discomfort, and the UFC assigned a doctor to my case, Michael 'Mick' Molloy. I had no reason to be overly worried. My assumption that I would be on the UFC Rotterdam card eventually came to fruition, and I was pencilled in to fight Willie Gates. This was a big fight but one that I felt I could definitely win if I got back to full health, particularly given the few months I had taken off.

Four weeks out from the fight I was in the SBG Concorde car park and my phone rang. It was Dr Mick Molloy. He discussed my back injury and told me that he was trying to organise an appointment for me to see a specific consultant. Then he mentioned that when he was going through my files, there was a note that there had been a haemophilia team present at my previous back surgery.

'Why were those guys there?' he asked me. In the back of my mind, I always knew this day would come. I felt a knot in my stomach but at the same time, a little weight lifted from my shoulders. I was sick of carrying the burden, and the added stress of trying to deal with everything going on in the gym was really weighing me down. Maybe I should have hung up the phone at that moment and thought about how I wanted to deal with the situation, but I didn't. I carried on the conversation even though I knew how severe the consequences could be. Never in human history had a haemophiliac competed at the top level of combat sports, and there was a reason for that; the risks were just too great. I knew right then that Dr Molloy's discovery would inevitably lead to the end of my career.

'What is this, Paddy? Why was Dr Ryan's team there when you were getting the surgery?'

In my head, logic told me that if the haemophilia team could be present during surgery and that was okay, then what would stop them being present outside the cage at my fights? If I could survive back and brain surgery, then surely I could fight. I knew that the minute I started to open up about my condition, I would be treated differently. I felt like I was walking on a beam across two buildings and if I didn't get to the other side, I'd fall and my career would be over, and with it, my life. I couldn't take that risk so I just didn't tell people about my blood condition. I had put eleven or twelve years into chasing this dream and I was going to do everything to continue to do so.

The most dangerous aspect of it all, for me, was not dying in the cage. It was my mental health. I knew what type of person I was and that I had struggled with my mental health for my entire life. There was no guarantee that I would come through the trauma of early retirement and that scared me. I cared about Tiernan and Chelsea so much. As Dr Molloy continued to ask questions, I just hoped that I would find the strength to handle whatever was about to come next. I stayed outside the gym and came clean.

'Listen, Mick. I have a blood disorder. It's technically not haemophilia. It's a Factor XIII deficiency. It doesn't affect my life, and I take fibrogammin for it every three weeks. I take care of it.'

When I first started taking fibrogammin, I was worried that the UFC would find it in my blood, but thankfully it didn't contravene any drug test regulations. The medication replaces a cell in my blood that dies and that's it. It increased my cell count to 60% of the normal level, and then eventually I was able to get it up to a normal person's level by changing the dosage. In my head, I felt safer than the average person because my blood levels were always being measured. In sparring, I never worried about it being dangerous or that I was close to death. It didn't cross my mind. I had a constant internal battle over whether I should just come clean and tell people. Ais knew about it, but that was it. Conor didn't know, Cathal didn't know, John didn't know. Even Chelsea didn't really know. Hiding made it harder, this secret of mine, but I knew I couldn't keep it hidden for ever. It was one of those things that was inside me and I needed to get it out at some point. When I came clean with Dr Molloy, I knew I had set fire to a fuse and there was little chance of it burning out quickly.

'I'm not your doctor, Paddy,' he explained. 'I'm employed by the UFC. I have a responsibility to share what you've just told me.'

'Hold on doctor, I've just told you something under doctor–patient confidentiality, so you can't just share it.'

His counter was simple. 'Well, Paddy, I can't sit beside a cage knowing that you're in there with haemophilia and not say anything about it. I would be liable for your death.'

'Then why don't you hand in your resignation so and get the fuck out of here?'

I may have overstepped the mark but I was 100% serious. I hung up the phone and walked into training, my career hanging by a thread. I was panicking and couldn't get it out of my head. I had to speak with John. He wasn't fully aware of my blood condition and we never had a proper conversation about it, but when I walked into the office that day, he could see something was up. I told him.

'Look, there's something coming down the hill and I just don't know if it will go away. It's to do with the blood disorder I have and I'm trying to deal with it with the UFC doctors but it doesn't look good. I think it might be alright but I'm very worried. I just want to let you know before it happens.'

I don't know whether John got scared about being liable for me, or if he was actually worried, but he was positive and reassuring at that moment.

'Let's not worry too much right now, Paddy. Let us see what happens and take it from there. There's no point in panicking now.'

I didn't want this blood condition. I never asked for it. When I first started fighting, it wasn't a case of me not telling people because I wanted to trick them or hide something. I just didn't want people to treat me differently, particularly John. I didn't want him to tell others not to train hard with me. I had found a sport that gave me everything I needed in life and I didn't want to risk losing that.

For two weeks, I heard nothing from the UFC. I bottled everything up and kept it inside me, even keeping it from Chelsea for as long as I could. I felt ashamed and didn't want to speak to people about my situation. As the days passed, I couldn't hide it any longer and came clean to Chelsea. I can't remember her exact reaction, but I do remember her being extremely supportive when I needed her most. She knew what fighting meant to me, and if risking everything was what I wanted to do, then there was no way she was going to stop me, so there was no point in being angry. I needed fighting. I needed risk. It's in me because of who I am.

While I was waiting for some sort of news, Dr Molloy — or Mick, as I was now calling him — was very helpful and even invited me out to his house one evening. I pulled up outside and he introduced me to his wife and children, who were playing in the garden. They were a lovely family and it took my mind off the inevitable conversation that awaited us. It also helped to gloss over the fact that I had told him to 'retire or fuck off' during our first phone call. We had spoken a few times since then and it was becoming clear to me that Mick was just a good family man that took his job seriously. I chatted to his kids, took some pictures and even signed some posters. I remember thinking to myself, 'This can only be a good thing, Paddy.' Mick was going to do everything he could to fight my corner, but if there was no solution and retirement was my only option, he was a man of strong enough principle to stand by that. I respected that from him and he was straight up with me from the start. We eventually got some privacy and began to discuss the elephant in the room.

'You're taking massive risks every time you enter that cage,' he told me. 'You could die in there from one punch.' I tried to plead my case, telling him that my blood level was under control thanks to the medication, but it was no use.

'Your body doesn't produce this factor, which makes you an extraordinary case. Not only that, you've factor XIII deficiency. It doesn't really exist, that's how rare it is.' The severity of it didn't matter to the doctor; the mere fact that it existed was enough. Once every three weeks, I injected myself with fibrogammin and that was it. When I was twelve years of age, I was taught how to inject myself and received a certificate in phlebotomy. I had been doing it for years.

Mick was straight up with me. 'I'm going to talk to the UFC and we're going to try to get this sorted.'

This had now escalated to the point where the UFC in Las Vegas was involved, and it was clear, one way or another, that the likelihood of me fighting again for the UFC was slipping away. An email eventually arrived from Las Vegas requesting me to send over a letter from my specialist saying that it was okay for me to continue to fight and that my blood condition did not have an effect on me fighting. Once I read that, my heart was crushed. I knew there was a very real probability that I would never fight again. Some people would have seen that email as a glimmer of hope, but I knew there was no way any specialist would put their reputation on the line by signing a letter like that. If I was a normal person and asked the doctor if I should go into a cage and fight another person, of course the answer would be no. No doctor would ever sign off on that being a good idea. The letter from the UFC told me two things: one, that they couldn't find a doctor to sign off; and two, I was now on my own and would have to begin searching for a specialist who would be willing to put their job on the line to help rescue my career.

My mind went into overdrive, processing everything but panicking at the same time. A mad thought entered my head, but one that could have solved my problem. How long would it take for me to qualify as a doctor? Could I sign my own waiver? I wanted this so badly that I would be willing to go to extreme lengths to prolong my career. Nothing was off the table at that point and I began making contact with doctors all over the world: Sweden, Switzerland, China. I just needed one to sign off. I googled as many specialists as I could and put a phone call in to each of them. A different person answered the phone each time, but the questions and inevitable answers remained the same.

'Would you say that I'm okay to fight?'

'No, I can't risk that.'

As the days passed, my chances slipped further and further away. The stress of it all was having a major effect on me and people began to take notice. I confided in those close to me in the hope that together we would find someone who could provide a positive outcome. I shared the UFC's email with a number of different specialists, asking their advice on how they would approach my situation, but I continued to hit dead ends. No doctor was willing to put their name on the line in order to allow a person with a serious blood disorder to fight in a cage in front of thousands of people. Factor XIII deficiency, due to its rarity, meant a lot of questions remained unanswered and no one was willing to go near it.

The one thing that kept me going was the fight with Willie Gates. All of the anguish and emotion was manifesting itself as hatred for this American fighter who I didn't even know. We all headed out to Iceland for camp a couple of weeks before my fight, including Conor, who was coming off the back of his first fight with Nate Diaz in March 2016. A rematch was mooted for the end of the summer and he was ready to right the wrongs of his defeat. A lot had changed since we first headed over to Mjolnir, particularly for Conor, who was now in a position to rent out a mansion for himself and the lads. I didn't want to get in the way of Conor's preparation, so I decided to rent my own apartment out there. That was important to me because I needed a space of my own, and also because the last time I was in Iceland, I was flat broke. Now, by getting my own place, I was able to fly Dylan Logan out with me and he could stay in the apartment too. Throughout my career, I made sure that I was helping the younger lads, trying to give them the experience to see what fighting at the top level is actually like. None of us had that opportunity when we were younger, and we felt it was our responsibility to make sure that the next generation did.

The apartment in Iceland was lovely and a far cry from the one I shared with the lads on my previous visit. There was a nice balcony, snow on the mountains and a good crew of us out there training. The relationship with Mjolnir had progressed to the point where we all felt united in our quest to become better martial artists. Things hadn't always been so rosy. During our first camps, there was a frostiness and awkwardness between us 'outsiders' and the Mjolnir residents. But the pointed stares had now changed to warm embraces and we were all on the same page. The minute we stepped into that gym, we were all teammates. I walked to the gym every morning. Although I was on my way to likely fight some vicious Icelandic Viking, those walks were when I felt most at ease. My life at the time was a walking paradox. To everyone on the outside, it seemed to be moving in the right direction and that I was on a one-way ticket to UFC gold, but to those who knew the real situation, things couldn't have been more precarious.

Throughout the camp, emails were being sent back and forth constantly, but every time I thought I'd jabbed my way forward, another crushing email would hook me right back. This was not going away. It was becoming more difficult to keep a level head, especially when I had decided it was best for me to begin to write my retirement speech. That was a strange feeling, almost like a fully healthy person starting to write their own eulogy.

That first week in Iceland, I was heading to the gym and working harder than ever before. I didn't care about my back injury. It didn't worry me at all. I kept going harder in every session and telling myself, 'This is what you're good at, Paddy. This is what you're meant to do. There's no way they'll let you go'. And I believed it too. I believed that if I worked harder and harder the UFC would do everything in their power to keep me on board. I tried everything to get the letter from a specialist clearing me to fight, but a glimmer of hope came from the one closest to me: my own doctor. He sent an email tip-toeing around the notion that he would support me. It wasn't a full declaration but it was something, and it was ten times more than anything else I had so I sent it to the UFC. The minute I pressed send, I could feel that bubble of anxiety in my stomach starting to expand. Every minute that passed felt like an hour, every hour felt like a day. Finally, a response came through. It wasn't enough. The UFC were clear; the letter was not sufficient, and they needed a doctor to fully sign off on my health. I sent the letter back, asking him to re-word it, and thoughts of forging the letter even entered my mind.

'I'm sorry, Paddy, I can't give you the full go-ahead,' he said. 'I don't know if you're ever going to be okay to fight again.'

'It's a fucking fight, doctor. We're getting in a cage and fighting. This is what I want.'

I knew deep down it was no good, though. No doctor worth their salt would sign Paddy Holohan's potential death warrant. I was in contact with the team doctor, Dan Healy, at the time too, but he had always been clear with me about the dangers I was meeting head on. Dan knew my chances were limited but did his utmost to help.

'That letter isn't good enough, Paddy,' Dan said. 'It needs to state explicitly that you are okay to fight and that the doctor consents to it.'

By now, Dan was in contact with John as both began to weigh up the situation. John was also in contact with Sean Shelby, the matchmaker from the UFC, keeping him in the loop. Once it had gotten to that point, though, I knew I had thrown my last punch in the UFC. Even in my own mind, I had come to accept defeat. To make matters worse, my back had stopped hurting me, and I was angry with myself for even reporting it to the UFC in the first place. All I needed was a little bit of rest, but I never pulled the handbrake. I was looking at six fights in less than two years, one every few months, and I would have fought even more if they came my way. I just wish someone had pulled me back and told me to rest and relax, but that winning feeling, the glory, is extremely addictive. That's just the way it is; being Paddy Holohan always seems to bring difficulties, even when I try to do the right thing.

I knew the UFC were protecting themselves and that I was collateral damage. I had to accept that I was also putting my opponents into risky situations. Nobody knows what impact my death at their hands could have had on their lives and it was selfish of me to always push that to the back of my mind. I don't regret it, though. I saw myself as having a disadvantage and I worked as hard as I could to reach my real potential and prove to myself that I was capable of incredible feats. The fighters who put performance-enhancing drugs in their body and punched others in the head didn't give a fuck, so why should I give a fuck about them? That's how I rationalised it. People were telling me to bow out, yet I could see PED users coming back from bans and being given a second chance, or in some cases, a third.

They were the rats who were playing with people's lives. I was only playing with my own.

As the inevitable edged closer, John and I decided we needed to sit down together. We met for Sunday brunch at the Vegamot, a bistro in Reykjavik, not too far from Mjolnir. It was the first time that John and I had sat down specifically to talk seriously and both of us knew why we were there. The walk down to meet John was bittersweet; it felt like the Last Supper, and although I was devastated at the thought of ending my career, I was relieved that I would finally get some closure. I just couldn't deal with the stress of it all any more. John had asked me to meet him, and I wasn't naive enough to think it was for a positive reason. I had been back and forth with letters, scurrying from specialist to specialist, sending barrages of emails in the hope that someone would rescue me from this nightmare, but by then, the decision had already been made by those in power. The fact that it was made without me meant it was even harder to swallow. A decision about me, without me; that's how I looked at it. Having given twelve years of my life to MMA, the full stop had been written on my career without even a phone call from the UFC.

'That's it, Paddy,' John said. 'It's over. Sean Shelby told me that you could die on the way up those steps to the cage. There is no way you can fight. I shouldn't even let you spar in the gym.' I sensed the irritation in his voice, but John was always so hard to read. I sensed he was upset too but couldn't be fully sure. I never lied to anybody. I just didn't want to be treated differently from everyone else.

'This is over, Paddy,' he said. 'The fight's not going ahead. You need to announce that you're retiring and the reasons why you are retiring.'

People might expect that we shed tears and reflected on my career with a heavy heart, but that wasn't the case. John wasn't the type to shed tears. We finished our conversation, went our separate ways and after that week he didn't make contact with me again until the opening of the gym a few months later. No hugs exchanged, no wisdom imparted, the chapter closed on the career of Paddy Holohan.

There was no way back. My career as a UFC fighter was over. The UFC gave me a couple of days to announce my retirement myself because they had to book a new opponent for Willie Gates. Before flying to Iceland, I knew there was a chance it could happen, but I still went because I hanging on to the hope of a miracle. In reality, I knew that there was always only going to be one outcome. I started to write my retirement message on my phone over the next couple of days. The mix of emotions flooded out: anger, relief, sadness, happiness, disappointment.

After my conversation with John, I went down to speak with Conor and the rest of the lads in the sauna. Conor's relationship with the UFC was becoming rocky and they weren't showing him the respect he deserved. They were trying to get him to fly from Iceland to Los Angeles to do a promotional gig, but he was getting tired of being dragged in all different directions.

'Do you know what, Paddy?' Conor said. 'I think I'm going to retire. Fuck them, I'm just going to tell them to fuck off.'

It was a strange moment. The two of us in a sauna in Iceland, seemingly with our whole careers ahead of us, but one of us was being forced to retire, and the other had decided to retire himself. I entered that sauna with the view of telling Conor and the others about my retirement but by the time we got dressed, it was Conor who had announced his to the world by sending his infamous 'thanks for the cheese' tweet. I didn't mind because it took the spotlight off me for a while. It even brought a little humour to a difficult situation because I felt that people probably wouldn't believe me now.

Later that day, I finally told the lads about my announcement. I didn't call them into a room and tell them I had something to announce. We were all on the battlefield and we didn't have time for that. I just waited for a moment when we were together.

'Lads, I'm going to have to retire. I have a blood condition and they won't let me fight any more.'

Their reaction was one of sadness and disbelief, and they just couldn't understand the suddenness of it all.

'You're after retiring now, Conor, and on Wednesday I actually have to retire,' I said jokingly.

'Oh fuck, sorry about that man.'

Conor's 'retirement' set the MMA world on fire. His tweet had been picked up everywhere and the world was talking about him. It took away the feeling I had that everyone was looking at me. I didn't want pity. I was still writing my retirement message, sending it back and forth to Chelsea for her advice, trying to capture all my emotions in the right words. The team were great. I was still training every day and they didn't change how they treated me. That was important for my morale. I didn't want to be excluded. Conor even contacted Dana White and told him he would un-retire and turn up to do the promotional event in LA if they let me fight the Willie Gates fight. That press conference was something that Conor did not want to do, and it contributed to a breakdown in his relationship with the UFC, but he was willing to go through with it just to help me.

'Let Paddy fight his next fight, and let him go out on his own terms.'

Conor never told me that he made that request to Dana, but I found out about it later and it meant a lot. I had said to him in private that all I wanted was to go out on my own terms, and he was willing to go to extreme lengths to make it happen. He didn't need to do that for me, particularly when he was going through so much stuff of his own, but he did, and that's the measure of a true friend. I would have loved the opportunity to fight Willie Gates, beat him, and then grab the microphone and tell people, 'That's all, folks', but life doesn't work like that. Instead, I have to spend the rest of my days dealing with the fact that my career ended on a loss.

Conor's retirement was short-lived, just two days in total. He settled his differences with the UFC and now it was time for me to make my announcement. I stared at that retirement message for three days and changed it hundreds of times. I knew what I had to do. There was a knot in my stomach that got worse and worse. I couldn't sleep. I told Tiernan what was happening and he barely flinched. He didn't care, he was just worried about his dad. That was the boost I needed. I was just his father to him and it didn't matter whether I was going to be a UFC fighter or not. I always knew the day would come and maybe that's why I brought Tiernan over to Boston with me, for fear that I'd never get the chance again. When I brought him to Glasgow, I remember arguing with Denise and telling her I didn't care, he had to be there. I knew it was never going to be for ever so I wanted to make the most of it for my son. I went on to Facebook, clicked publish, and threw my phone on the ground. I was heartbroken that something I loved had been taken away from me, but I also felt a strange sense of relief.

The reaction, as expected, was one of disbelief throughout the MMA world. People thought that I was joking at first. 'What's going on? Is there something in the air in Iceland with these retirements?' I tried not to get bogged down in the reaction but I couldn't stay away from my phone. I had a week left in Iceland and, to be honest, it was perfect as it allowed me to come to terms with the end of my career without the spotlight of the media shining brightly on me. Floods of messages started to pour in. The comments from all over the world were hugely positive and that's something that made me proud. Respect and honesty were two important characteristics to me, and the response I received showed me that people understood that. People understood that I had a tough life but kept on grafting, and I think that's what earned me respect.

Not for the first time, Conor was really there for me. When the UFC was tearing my life apart, Conor was keeping it together. It's in moments like that that you truly realise who's there to support you. Chris Fields, Tom King, even Robbie Keane, they all reached out to help me with sincerity.

We ended up getting a day off from the training camp, so Conor and I decided to head out to a remote horse ranch with some of the Icelandic fighters. It was one of the best days of the trip and exactly what I needed at that time. We rode the horses out to a secret natural lagoon and stayed there for hours. Staring up at the stars, it was the perfect tonic for what I was going through. Someone broke out a few cheap cans of beer and we relaxed, taking it all in. We had come so far in our careers, yet at that moment, it was still the simple things that gave us the most pleasure. My career was coming to an end while Conor's was continuing to skyrocket, but here we were, still the same two Dublin young fellas looking to have some fun.

We headed back to Dublin a few days later, and I bade farewell to Iceland. I didn't know if I'd ever return. I left Ireland as a UFC fighter and returned as an unemployed twenty-nine-year-old. A new challenge in my life had presented itself and I knew I would be facing the biggest fight of my career. I don't think I was depressed arriving back to Dublin, but I definitely wasn't myself. I had the Tallaght gym and I was looking forward to getting stuck into it fully, even if it was proving to be a nightmare. Opening a gym had always been in my plans. It would be my legacy. Careers are often short-lived, but I felt a responsibility to the people of Tallaght. I had tried everything to fix the problems inside my head — alcohol, drugs, one-night stands — but none of it worked quite like martial arts.

When UFC Rotterdam came around, Willie Gates had a new opponent and I had to watch that fight knowing that I would have won. In the space of two weeks, I had lost my career, my livelihood and, of course, €4,000. People forget that side of it. I had a camp that I had to pay for, expenses associated with preparing for my fight, and I had trained for zero money for weeks, but once the fight was taken away from me, I lost it all. No phone call, no support from the UFC, just a thank you and goodbye. I never received a pension or a cheque from the promotion thanking me for the value I had added over the couple of years I fought under their banner. A year's wage, gone in an instant. I took a photo outside the Tallaght gym and posted it to social media: 'When one door closes, another one opens.'

Paddy Holohan, 12-2 — 2007–2015

Retirement felt like a death, but I just didn't know how to grieve. Some days I was okay, feeling fine, but then it would all come down on me like a ton of bricks and I wouldn't even be able to get out of my bed. My entire life's workings had been ripped apart and I would never ever get them back. I lay in bed for days on end and didn't know what else to do. I lost my purpose and direction. No future, no career. There was nothing to work towards. I had always lived my life at 100 miles per hour, but it had come to an abrupt halt. Some days I would wake up, reflect on my career with a positive mindset, and get on with my life. But other days I was paralysed by the anxiety and heartbreak of having to restart my life again. I didn't turn to drink or drugs because I knew there would be no coming back if I did. If I lit that fuse, it would have resulted in disastrous consequences for myself and my family. I was left with a decision to keep on fighting, or just submit to the pressure and pain of it all. And that second option scared me. My entire life I had somehow pulled myself up after hitting the floor. I knew I was of no use to anyone in bed. The only option was to channel every ounce of energy into making the Tallaght gym the best I could and getting my life back on track.

I knew people were talking about me too, watching for any reaction, trying to see what was going on in my head and whether I was able to deal with the blow of retirement. My entire life I had overcome the preconceptions and paths already laid out for me, and there was no way I was going to just throw all that away now. For all the negativity of the situation, I knew I had a responsibility, not only to myself and my family but to the people of Jobstown. I had become a guiding light for so many people in the area, proof that you can achieve your goals, and it would have had a detrimental effect on my own people had I decided to just give up on everything. I have an addictive personality. I know there's a part of me that I can't control. Throughout my life, I had been addicted to something: pain in my youth, alcohol and drugs, MMA, my relationship with Chelsea. Now that fighting was gone, I had to be extra careful that it wasn't replaced by one of the ghosts of my past.

People expected me to hit the floor, but that wasn't me. Self-pity can be addictive for some people, they enjoy the notion of people feeling sorry for them, but not me. I was a council estate kid with a chip on my shoulder and I hated it when people felt pity towards me. I had a chance to rise back up and prove people wrong. Although I was crushed inside, I put on a happy face and started to get on with things as best I could.

When we finally managed to get a building for the gym, it was in nothing like turnkey condition, and I worked with a local councillor, Cathal King, to change its use in order to get permission to run a gym. Behind the scenes, there was a new disagreement every day. It was clear that the lads needed me, but my newly formed paranoia meant I kept wondering for how long? I eventually spoke to John about how I was feeling, and his advice was comforting.

'Sure fuck it, Paddy. If it all goes wrong, just go down the road and open up your own gym. I'll help you out. I'll back you up.'

John reassured me at a time when I was really struggling. This gym was supposed to be my pension, not my penance. The Tallaght gym had my name all over it, and I couldn't afford to let it fail. I had been working on the gym for four months by now without a single penny being sent my way. I kept asking about my wage and was met with the same answer — 'You'll be paid next month, Paddy' — but I didn't hold my breath.

The madness of the gym situation was beginning to take over my life, but training offered me an escape. I took every last drop of energy I had and put it into getting the gym ready for business; laying mats, building bathrooms, plastering the walls. I grafted and grafted, essentially working as an unpaid labourer, until it was ready.

The opening day of the Tallaght gym eventually came around and I had put in countless hours, working around the clock, to ensure it was going to be ready. I called in every favour I ever had with the people of Tallaght. I put all the mats down with Joey Breslin, a lifelong teammate of mine at SBG. I brought down painters to put up a massive mural on the wall with a number of fighters, including one of me with the head of a gorilla and the flag in the air, a throwback to my night in Glasgow. I organised barbecues, bouncy castles, entertainers. This was a day for my community. TV3, one of the main TV stations in the country, was there recording a documentary about me called *This Is Jobstown*. Hundreds of people turned up for the opening, including Conor, and I was proud of the show of support I had received.

We grew the gym to over 200 members but things were still crazy beneath the surface. The problems kept mounting with every new disagreement. It was important for me to treat people the SBG way, with respect, and help them to fulfil their potential and get something back from martial arts, but not everybody involved in running the gym had the same priorities. Training was difficult, sleep was nonexistent, and I was struggling to pull myself out of bed. The situation threatened to finally erupt and a meeting was called between everybody involved. Either we sorted out all our disagreements so that we could move forward together, or I would walk away from the gym.

Conor came to the meeting to help me fight my corner. He had more money than anyone in the room, including the main investor, and made it clear that he would back me financially if things continued spiralling out of control. In the end, we came to an agreement that listed everyone's respective titles, with the following understanding: we made a list of all of the ongoing issues and the areas that needed to improve, and if the investors didn't resolve them, the gym could not move forward as a business. We signed the document, hoping for a fresh start, but nothing changed.

Conor's life was going in a number of different directions at breakneck speed at the time. He was flying all over the world and despite becoming the first 'Champ-Champ' in UFC history, he still made time for me. He was the only one who kept making sure I was okay. One night we decided to meet up at Tallaght Stadium, the home of Shamrock Rovers Football Club. Conor, Charlie Ward and myself sat down the back in one of Conor's jeeps, having a conversation about the gym and the best thing for me to do.

'I can't just leave, Conor,' I told him. 'If I walk straight out of the building, it will let so many people down. Some will have nowhere to go, and will need to stay there, while others will leave. If I go, I need to have a building ready, so I can bring the people with me.'

Conor's reaction was unexpected, but I had learned to expect that from him over the years. He picked up the phone and called his manager, Audie Attar.

'Audie, if I was to get a UFC-quality gym in this town next week, what's it going to take? See that gym we put up in Vegas, I want to put something similar in Tallaght.'

I couldn't believe what I was hearing.

'I'll give €150,000 towards it, Audie,' he added.

'Conor, I don't have that kind of money,' I told him.

'Don't you fucking worry, Paddy. I've got your back. I'd give you that money tomorrow and that would be it. You don't owe me anything, ever.'

That was typical of Conor; always loyal, dedicated and supportive of me. He's one of the realest motherfuckers there is. He was under no obligation to do that for me, no obligation to even meet with me. He had the eyes of the world on him at that time and was busy chasing one of the biggest fights in combat history with Floyd Mayweather, but still stood side by side with me and fought my case. I was drowning and he was there to rescue me.

'Yeah, yeah, we'll suss it out. We'll ring people now,' Audie said. The gym looked like a real possibility, and with Conor's backing, I could have a gym up in no time. Conor's support helped to build up my self-esteem again, and for the first time in a while, my confidence returned.

'You're right, Conor,' I said. 'I am stronger than them. I am the gym.'

'Fucking right, Paddy. You're everything in there. That's a shell of a building. Now use that and go back and get things sorted in there.'

I was being suffocated in the gym, yet every time I texted John, he would respond with a thumbs up. Either that, or he wouldn't even text back. I was fed up with it and organised a sit down with him in his consultation room, the very same room where we had spoken initially about the opportunity in the Tallaght gym.

'John, I'm thinking of walking away from the gym,' I explained. 'I can't take it any more. It's affecting my daily life and nothing has changed. It's just constant stress.'

'Paddy, relax. Give it one more shot, and if it all doesn't work out, you and Chelsea leave and set up another gym.'

John always had the ability to calm me down, and I went from a position of definitely leaving to considering giving it one more shot.

'I'm going mental, John. I want to have a kid with Chelsea. I need some stability. I don't want to wake up every single day dreading getting out of bed and coming into work. I want to build something special. I want to build a house, look after my ma. She's not doing too well.'

I opened up to John but his response was the same as ever, 'Paddy, just one more shot. We'll get everything sorted. If it doesn't work out, go up the road and rent a gym. Call it SBG Belgard and I'll back you.'

It was like music to my ears. John was finally on board and willing to back me if things didn't improve.

'Brilliant,' I said. 'I have my own money, my own plan. I just need you to support me.'

We shook hands and I left the room with a smile. It was as if a huge weight had been lifted off my shoulders, but I was foolish to think it would last.

Nothing changed. The antics at the gym continued and one night after a long day in the gym, the investors called me into the office and asked me to go home to sack Chelsea because of 'cutbacks'. The gym was thriving, despite everything that was going on in the background, and this was the straw that broke the camel's back. Just like that, I walked out of the Tallaght gym for good.

I don't for a second regret walking out that day and opening my own gym. I set myself free and from that moment, things started to feel right for once. This was Tallaght, this was D24, this was my area. When I started off, no one in Tallaght knew what MMA stood for or what the UFC was. I advocated for that to change. I was the one scurrying around Tallaght looking for buildings for the gym. I had put my heart and soul into it before it even opened its doors. All I wanted was a secure and simple life with enough to provide for my family. There was no way I wasn't going to have a gym in Tallaght.

That night I turned up back at the house and Chelsea was awake, waiting for me. She had phoned ten or eleven times and knew something was up when I wasn't answering.

'We're out. We're out of the gym. We're going to build our own and finally do what we should have done a long time ago.'

Chelsea was in shock but I was delighted inside. Plenty of people who should have been fighting my corner simply were not. I had finally stood up for myself. I was out on my own, afraid of what the future might hold for Chelsea, Tiernan and me, but I was proud of how I had acted. I needed to know my worth and rebuild my self-esteem. That night, Chelsea came up with the name 'SBG Dublin 24', the postcode for Tallaght.

The investors released a statement that evening to say that there was a 'staffing issue' and 'senior management' had made a decision to part ways with Paddy Holohan. The next day, I woke up and made it public through a social media post that I had left the Tallaght gym.

'As of Tuesday 21st February 2017, I am not in anyway connected with SBG Tallaght on the Belgard Road,' I wrote. 'I will not be teaching any classes, be connected to any programmes or advertising related to it. In relation to the aforementioned "Staffing Issues" I would never terminate someone's employment who was part of the SBG Tallaght's plan before anyone else. Loyalty is key to me. I apologise to all my students for the inconvenience of changing my location, but I am still fully committed to my plan to improve our area with SBG martial arts programmes. I have located a temporary place from next week to train and plan to continue what we started until we secure a permanent home for SBG D24 which myself and Joey Breslin will take charge of. Lots of people have been asking questions regarding the status of their membership carrying over. The answer is no. We will be a separate club but still operating in Tallaght.'

The response was hugely positive towards me, and for that I was so grateful, but there was a lot of anger and negativity towards the Tallaght gym and towards John in particular. Orlagh, John's partner, contacted Chelsea and told her that the backlash was really hurting him and that he couldn't eat or sleep. Two days later, we were in Belfast for a fight and John called me over.

'Listen, all of this stuff going down with the gym, I just want to make sure the two of us are alright.' It felt weird to me from the start because it was the first time I had really seen John acting as open as that.

'Will you put a post up to say the two of us are cool because I just want to set the record straight?' he asked. I agreed, wanting to just move forward with my life, so we took a selfie and I posted it to social media.

'A few things to clear up after this week,' I wrote. 'Me and The Coach have and always will be cool. SBG Tallaght was an invested project separate to John Kavanagh's SBG Ireland gym and he had no decision in me parting. "SBG Tallaght Senior Management" is an investor. Not John Kavanagh or any other SBG coach or fighter. I have no quarrel with SBG, and my team stand behind me and my decision.'

I've stared at that image countless times, and John's face paints an interesting picture. The stress he was feeling was obvious, an indication that the fallout was continuing to have an effect on him. I drove to Dublin after the event, slept in my car for an hour, and then flew to Liverpool to corner Richie Smullen for a Shinobi event with John. John barely acknowledged the social media post, didn't share, didn't comment. Now the people of Tallaght were off his back, John was back to being John. He claimed he was caught in the middle, and was technically 'cool' with me, but he certainly wasn't helping. People questioned my loyalty to John, feeling that he had clearly screwed me over, but I was still willing to support him. I just didn't see it at the time as clearly as I do now.

Within a week or so, Chelsea and I had set up a temporary gym in the local leisure centre in Tallaght with the support of my friends and those who had been coaching in the Tallaght gym with me. We got mats, rented the hall and created a timetable for classes. I was on the hunt for a building throughout that time and just hoped that people would support me. And that they did. On the first night of classes in that leisure centre, almost 100 people arrived to show their support. I was overwhelmed by the response. Everyone, including the likes of Artem Lobov, shared messages of support. 'There's only one place to train in Tallaght' was the message everyone was spreading, but John wasn't happy. He even contacted Artem and told him, 'Stay neutral in this,' essentially telling some of my teammates and friends to stay on the sidelines. It was sad to see how our relationship had changed.

I was fighting so many battles at that time and those who stood by me know who they are. Artem, Conor, Roddy, Chris Fields, Tom King – they all supported me. The search for the new building continued, and Chelsea and I saw places of all different shapes and sizes. Although John and I had drifted apart, we were still on speaking terms, and I sent him pictures of buildings I was looking at. I had previously viewed a bike shop that definitely had potential to be transformed into something.

'Don't even bother going to view the big building up the road, take that smaller bike shop. I know which one I'd prefer to train in – a gym run by a former UFC fighter, or a fancy one with no coaches', said John.

John had almost convinced me, and I was set to ring the landlord to cancel the viewing, but changed my mind at the last second. It would prove to be one of the most important decisions of my life. When I viewed the bigger place, I fell in love. It was a massive building, 10,000 square feet with two storeys, and would need plenty of work, but the foundations and the structure of the building suited perfectly. I could see immediately that the potential was there to build something special, even if it did take a bit of convincing to get Chelsea to fully buy into the place. The minute I set eyes on it, my mind went into overdrive visualising how it could look. I could see mats, walls, bags, posters, belts hanging on the wall, a cage. I was awestruck.

'This can go here! That can go there! We've found it, Chelsea! We've found it!'

This was going to be the home of SBG Dublin 24. It was €300 a month more expensive than the bike shop but had ten times the potential, so I signed the lease as quickly as I could. John was away a lot due to Conor's camp for the Mayweather fight, but when he found out about the gym and heard that I signed for the bigger building, he was livid. He continued to advise me to go with the smaller bike shop, but his agenda had become compromised in my head, so there was no way I was going against my gut.

'You're going to need €100,000, Paddy,' he told me. 'It's too much risk.'

Later that day, I received a text message from John's phone that suggested I should change the name of the gym to 'Holohan's' and remove the SBG. For me, that was a non-runner. I had earned my slice of the SBG brand and now John was trying to push me further out the gate.

'No, John,' I said. 'This is it, I'm going for it.' And that's when everything took another turn.

'Paddy, we're going to have to discuss the reality that there's now going to be three SBGs within five miles of each other,' he said.

'Hold on. When I was looking for buildings, this area was okay, John. You also told me the lads in the Tallaght gym had their chance and you were now going to help me. What's changed?'

We all built that brand. It was a name on a door in the gym in Rathcoole all those years ago that no one knew about until we marched it into the cage time and time again. I put that SBG gorilla on my ass and stormed into some of the most dangerous situations imaginable. I told him, 'If you want to just leave me here and do your own thing, not talking to me or helping me, then fine, but SBG Dublin 24 is staying.'

Hail, rain or snow, I was down in that gym working throughout the night getting it ready for the opening. We were still running classes in the leisure centre, but had expanded to a local spin studio too, so the pressure was on to get the new building ready. We took a photo on the first day of the Tallaght gym, and a year later, 90% of the same people were still with me in the new SBG Dublin 24. That was true loyalty. We all went through the transition together. Jim Donnelly, who built all the SBG gyms, helped me out massively. I was sleeping in the building some nights too, doing everything I possibly could to get the place ready. Blood, sweat, tears, fears, hopes, dreams, those were the foundations of SBG Dublin 24. Conor was in contact with me throughout and his support kept me motivated. Fightstore helped me too. So did Simon McEvoy, the strength and conditioning coach in SBG Concorde, who offered to help out with the entire strength and conditioning programme. Simon had plans to rent an area in SBG Dublin 24 from me to train the junior coaches, but would still remain as a coach in SBG Concorde. It seemed like a nice fit but John blew a gasket. He was furious and looked at the situation as if I was trying to poach a coach. He also felt that I had taken Joey Breslin away from SBG, but the truth was that Joey Breslin hadn't coached for John in over four years and left the Tallaght gym at the same time I did.

John should have come into SBG Dublin 24 and helped me with the gym, while also helping the investors with the Tallaght gym. I wouldn't have had a problem with that. Whether he was able to help me or not, he should have said it straight out, rather than removing himself from the situation. When John was starting off, everybody helped him. Jim Donnelly physically built his gyms, I helped John, Conor helped John, so too did Cathal, Gunnar, Ais, and Artem. Everyone played their part, and that's what you do in a successful team. You help each other. Instead, he left me on my own. Weeks later, he sent me a message saying, 'Listen, I'm busy. You're busy. I suggest you concentrate on doing you, and I'll concentrate on doing me. We can both go our separate ways.' It was heart-breaking. I didn't text back, partly because I didn't know what to say, but mostly because I was sad that our relationship had deteriorated to such a low.

I couldn't afford to dwell on the end of our relationship. The open day arrived quickly and it was a massive success. Conor was away on a fight camp at the time, but he turned up when he was back and surprised a class of teenagers. They were in awe of him. My whole community stood up and supported me on that open day. I always felt like if I ever fell, Tallaght would be there to catch me. All of the worries of building the gym were off my back and we were now ready to open the doors. I had spent so much time making sure everything was regulated and up to scratch: the use of the building, fire safety, health and safety procedures. I scrutinised every single box and made sure I ticked them all off one by one. By the time we were done, I had spent all of my earnings on the gym, poured them into my dream, and was left with €1,000 in my account. My fishing rod was most certainly in the water and I had no choice but to make sure I caught something big.

After branching out on our own, Chelsea and I were on a mission. When we left the Tallaght gym, we found ourselves in a situation where we had no jobs. My pride was dented and I was hurt badly, worried that maybe she would start to think I wasn't the guy she first thought I was and leave. All of those insecure thoughts ran through my mind. I had gone from a strong, warrior fighter to a retired, jobless bum. But she stuck with me and I worked even harder. My pride was dented but my will to succeed only strengthened. People often ask me what makes me different and I always give the same answer. I've been through the bullshit, I've been fucked over, but I've remained the same person and that's what makes me powerful. I'm not the bullied person who becomes a bully; I'm the person who learns from being bullied and makes sure to avoid acting like that. I forgive. I give a hand up.

There was a massive influx of people from the Tallaght gym and within six months we had grown to over 350 members. Most people who come to train in mixed martial arts will never fight, nor do they want to fight. The focus is on a better way of life, learning the values, discipline, building up your confidence. Chelsea and I created a place for families and kids, as well as elite fighters, similar to the team environment in which I had flourished. John's gym was previously called Ultimate Fitness Centre, but he quickly changed it to Family Martial Arts Centre. Yes, it was an SBG gym, but the sign above the building put the emphasis on the familial aspect of martial arts.

After a few months, a group event was organised by John Kavanagh and Matt Thornton which summoned all SBG gyms in Ireland to a meeting in the Sheldon Park Hotel, Dublin. Owen Roddy and Tom King were all there. The purpose of the meeting was to introduce an annual €5,000 fee for all SBG gyms in return for business advice, social media support and affiliation with the SBG brand. This was the first time I had heard of a fee and I felt myself and the other veterans in the room had done enough for the brand. We had paid our dues with blood, sweat and tears over the previous ten years. The meeting went on for hours with little progress, but my mind was made up; there was no way I was paying the €5,000. It wasn't about the money, it was about more than that. I told John flat out that there was no way I was paying and I switched my focus back to SBG Dublin 24.

John spent the next few days meeting with all the gym owners, including me. When he called, I thought it was to resolve the situation, but as we sat in the No Shame studio upstairs in the SBG Dublin 24 gym, it was clear that he was here to reiterate the importance of the €5,000 fee. On the advice of those close to me, I offered to pay €2,000 per year and to teach classes in SBG Concorde to show my loyalty, but it was refused. It hurt to see what our relationship had become but I had to stand up for myself. My interests were clearly not a concern of John's. We decided to go our separate ways.

Chelsea and I threw everything into the gym and never looked back. I'm fortunate to be in the position I'm in now, but do I miss fighting? Yes, I miss it like hell. I miss it so badly, but I'm older now. When I was younger, I had nothing to lose and that's what made me fearless. I was okay with dying; me and God were good. But when Tiernan, Chelsea, and eventually little Séamus Patrick Holohan came on the scene, my perspective on survival changed drastically. When you've something to lose, you'll do anything to stay alive.

Séamus's birth had a profound effect on me. I was nervous and excited in equal measure when Chelsea went into labour and we raced to the Coombe Hospital, the same hospital in which I was born thirty-one years earlier. It felt like my life had come full circle. The moment Séamus entered the world the planet came to a standstill. Everything stops as you watch a new life begin. Chelsea's strength and power humbled me as I watched her transform from my girlfriend into the mother of my child. I took my top off as the midwife handed Séamus to me, and placed him against my chest. I could feel his heartbeat sync with mine. Our family had grown to four.

I've matured with my age and I'm no longer just Paddy; I'm a father to two beautiful sons. I fought to forge a better life for Tiernan and Séamus, and I accomplished that mission.

Two years have passed since we first opened SBG D24 and I'm proud to say that 90% of the people who started with me are still with us today. Loyalty is rare and it's an amazing experience knowing you're having a positive influence on people every day and watching them fulfil their potential. It's been a whirlwind of a journey, but the gym keeps increasing and improving every month. I've been coaching for twelve years now and I've learned so much about myself and about other people. I could have laid down, I could have given up and ended up sitting on the high stool in some pub in Jobstown, but I didn't. I never stopped and I don't plan on stopping any time soon. I went from fighting in the UFC to retirement, to then sticking myself in a rocket and shooting myself into the next stage of my life. I just didn't know that rocket would end up landing me at the polling stations.

Jobstown rogue, UFC fighter, Dublin businessman — now it was time for Paddy Holohan, the politician, to take the stage and face the biggest fight of his life.

CHAPTER 15 ....

When you put people into a furnace, it can either melt them or forge them. I'm the latter. Every setback made me stronger.

By thirty years of age, I had accomplished a lot. I was a UFC veteran, I had fought a main event on the world's premium MMA promotion, and I was the first Irishman to get a UFC victory on home soil. What matters most to me, however, is that I'm respected and I've stayed true to myself through it all. I never ripped off anyone, not even the people who were trying to screw me. It didn't change me and I'm still the same Paddy Holohan, just smarter than I was before.

I came through so much adversity and when I was thrown overboard, I didn't just swim to the surface, I sped to dry land and rebuilt my life. My focus switched from chasing money to influencing change. I'm after something bigger than monetary value now. I'm establishing my legacy, and promoting the value of helping people and not looking for anything in return. I just want to help people, my own people, and that's why I decided to run for election in my local constituency

Cathal King has always been a person I've admired. In life, in politics, he's been a beacon of success for the people of Tallaght, spending well over a decade as an elected representative and even achieving the honorary title of Lord Mayor of Tallaght for a period. Cathal had always been good to me throughout my struggles, helping me with planning permission for the gym among other things. When I confided in Cathal that I was working on a book, I read him an extract and he was moved immediately. I spoke to him about my life growing up, about Belfast and about my career, and he hung on my every word.

'This is supposed to happen, Paddy. You've got to keep going. Would you ever consider running for election?'

My response was as swift as one of my jabs.

'One hundred per cent.'

Having been involved in and flying the flag for my community for a number of years, getting involved in politics was an opportunity I couldn't refuse. I felt a responsibility to the people of Tallaght, and Jobstown in particular, to show them the potential that exists in all of us with the right combination of a positive mindset and a desire to succeed. When I signed up for the election, I knew I was putting myself on the frontline for a five-year term if I was elected. To be quite honest, I didn't know there was a salary, even if the €18,000 was less than the minimum wage. As an elected representative, there's a responsibility to be available to the people 24/7, and anyone financially motivated is in the wrong game. I'm in it for the right reasons. I want to effect change, I want to provide people with hope, I want to help.

When I announced that I was running in the Tallaght South constituency for the Sinn Féin party, the response was one of positivity and support, coupled with the usual Irish begrudgery.

'Sure what does he know about politics? What changes can he make?'

Like so many times before, people wrote me off before ever giving me a chance to prove myself. They should have known better. I didn't indulge in any dirty politics or mud-slinging. I stayed true to my word, listened to the grievances of my people and put everything I had into becoming the best politician I possibly could be.

The campaign trail hotted up eight weeks out from polling day and it felt longer than any training camp I had endured in my previous career. At least in that scenario, you can control certain aspects. In politics, I couldn't. It was relentless, draining and motivating. I spent days on end knocking on doors, running away from dogs, being chased by kids and being greeted with all kinds of welcome. We knocked on every single door in Jobstown. One or two answered with a 'fuck off', others with a scream, but some answered with a smile and that made it all worthwhile. I met some of the kindest people, pouring their hearts out to me on their doorsteps about problems they shouldn't have been experiencing, things that were out of their control. That was when I knew I had to do something, and it motivated me to work even harder. I felt a responsibility to help those who couldn't help themselves. I was used to being in the gutter and I always wanted someone to help me, but now that I was in a position to help others, it was vital that I made the most of it. Oscar Wilde once said, 'We're all in the gutter, but some of us are looking at the stars.' That was me. I've always felt a responsibility to the people of Jobstown, and to represent the area as best I could. I know I can't come in and change the world, but what I can do is make a start. I've already got 150 kids in my gym and I'm using MMA to help them in the same way it helped me. It's helping them to learn vital skills that they can apply to life. I can show them that the gangster way of life is no way to live and only leads to hardship and pain.

When I was eighteen years of age, Tiernan was born. That moment gave me the energy to propel myself into the UFC. I didn't look back, I stuck my blinkers on and kept going. When I was forced into retirement, I dragged myself out of the gutter and drove forward. When I lost the gym, I was facing the lowest point of my life, depressed and unemployed, but I dragged myself out of that hole too and now here I was with a real chance of being elected by my own people and becoming the first democratically elected male UFC fighter in history by doing so.

Election day arrived, and after a tough few months of canvassing, it was finally time for the people to have their say. I had a busy day ahead of me helping people get to the polling stations, so I set off knocking on doors and explaining to people the importance of using their vote.

'Come on, you're getting into the jeep and we're going to make a difference.'

Some agreed and I drove them down to the polling station. I had lifts organised for old women on my road and drove them down personally, too. I drove down their daughters, and even ferried young lads from my housing estate who had never voted in their life down to the polling station. I did everything I could and it all counted. I walked into the polling station and the person working there said to me, 'There's a lot of your people voting, lads in tracksuits that have never voted before.' Besides asking what he meant by 'my people', I was proud that I had helped people to understand the importance of their vote and the difference it can make. This was about making my sons' lives better, my housing estate better, and the future for my people better.

I poured every ounce of energy into making sure that everyone who had said they would vote for me actually did. I drove around my housing state from the early hours of the morning all the way up until 9.30pm that night, ferrying people to the polling station. I turned up at people's doors, caught people down by the shops, and on one occasion, even grabbed a lad out of his bed. Every single vote was important and I made sure that I got as many as I could. Some of them didn't even know how to vote, and for many, it was their first time, but I was there to help them. By voting, it gives me an opportunity to show them what voting means and how it can impact change. If you vote for me, I will die for you and do everything I can to improve your life. As an elected councillor, you can see who has voted and who has not voted. It's not possible to see who they voted for, but at least it allows me to differentiate between the people who said they would vote and the people who actually went to the trouble of voting. I would still help those who didn't vote, but the ones who did would be top of my list of helping people. My main goal was to affect change and help to improve people's lives, and the people who voted for me are the ones that gave me a chance to do so.

Of all the votes, the one that made me most proud was that of my mother. My relationship with my mother was always a difficult one, but one in which we loved each other dearly. I was bursting with pride as we walked out of the house that morning to vote.

'Who will we vote for?' my mother asked.

'Me!' I laughed.

It was the first time in my life that I could physically see that my mother was proud of me. She was smiling from ear to ear. She takes things day by day and nothing seems to faze her, positively or negatively, but that day it was different. I could sense her pride heading to the polling station. Even in the car, she was the one initiating the conversation, whereas it was always the opposite for the previous thirty years. She even told me how she had told her taxi driver that her son was running in the election. I was a million miles from being elected at that stage, but politics had already brought my mother and me closer than we had ever been. It was a powerful moment and I was now the one with the smile on my face. She raised me in a single-parent household, with limited opportunities and a basic education, but here she was, on the way to vote for her son in the local elections.

People often have perceptions about the type of person who grows up in a council estate, that they're nobodies and destined for certain failure, but very often these people can rise up and become someone special through pure grit and determination. They can become firefighters, doctors, gardaí, and that's why it's important to give everyone an equal opportunity to flourish. People want results now, but for me, it's all about playing the long game and making lasting change. Jobstown has its good and bad aspects, but I can communicate with its people because I'm one of them. Sometimes they're just confused or have become lost in life and try to carry on without hope. If you take away someone's hope, you have to be very careful about what happens because hope is something that everyone needs, regardless of their demographic or social class. If these young fellas grow up like I did, with very little hope, then there's no chance for Jobstown to develop, and its people will never make it.

As the day wound down, I went home knowing that my fate was completely out of my hands and I had to trust that the people of Jobstown made the right decision. It was a difficult feeling to grapple with, trying to control the uncontrollable, and completely alien to my experiences in the cage, where I could physically make something happen with my own hands. When I was fighting, I could work on certain techniques, certain game plans, but when it comes to public elections, there was nothing I could do except wait. In this form of combat, there was no transition to fight mode, no moment where I could launch at my opponent and throw everything into it, and that certainly didn't help me to get to sleep any easier that night. The votes were cast on Friday and the count was due to commence the following morning.

When I woke up on the morning of the count, it wasn't too dissimilar to the morning of a fight. Boom. Fully awake just like that. I grabbed Chelsea and baby Séamus and headed off into the unknown. When we arrived, an overwhelming feeling of emotion came over me as I saw my face on a ballot paper with the number one written next to it. The significance of each and every single vote was not lost on me, and each one was an indication of people placing their trust in my ability to improve their lives.

Watching the votes being counted was an amazing but infuriating process. I could feel the dopamine surging through my brain as each vote for Holohan appeared in front of my eyes. Holohan. Holohan. Holohan. Piles of them gathered on the table. People voted for me in their droves and although that filled me with pride, it was also disappointing to know that certain people didn't vote for me. Regardless of the outcome, there was still work to do. I understood the significance of my potential election to office, breaking the mould of political dynasties and families being voted in. I wanted to become a lightning rod of hope for young people in Tallaght and prove to them that anything is possible, that they could achieve whatever they set their mind to. I started in the basement of life and experienced a more than difficult childhood. If I could get through those tough times, turn things around and get elected by my own people, then there's no reason why anyone else couldn't.

Keeping my cool throughout the count was extremely hard. I came face to face with other politicians, politicians who had completely neglected the needs of the people of my housing estate, yet there they were, parading themselves around the count stations in Citywest. One in particular had tried to evict a neighbour of mine just a week earlier and had cut funding for mental health services but had the audacity to stroll around like the Queen of Sheba. It helped me to notice that there were people running in these elections who were perceived as model citizens and public figures when in reality they were ruthless and soulless. As much as that angered me, I knew I would have to keep my cool and focus on the task at hand. In politics, there are very few swift jabs or leg sweeps. For me to achieve my goals and to forge a better life for the people of my community, it would take discipline, patience and drive. So I turned my back and tried to ignore the self-anointed royalty behind me. My time to make a change would come.

Another aspect of the count that I struggled with was seeing the disappointment on people's faces as it became apparent that they were not being elected. These were good people, people who would do anything for their housing estates, yet the support they had given was not reciprocated. The first unofficial count had me in good stead, thankfully. It said that I had come out on top, but the fact that it was unofficial did nothing to help my nerves. The count had me at about 900 first preference votes, which would leave me needing another 100 to reach the quota and become elected.

The competitive streak in me came to the fore, because being elected wasn't good enough for me any more. I was now fixated on topping the poll. That would send out a real message. My running mate, Louise Dunne, helped me so much with the campaign, and although she had a battle ahead of her, there was still every chance she would be elected. Cathal King, the man who made the election happen for me, sailed through in his own constituency of Tallaght Central, being elected with ease, so things were looking good. Although my votes were flooding in, it was still disappointing to see how many people had placed their faith in the sitting government of Fine Gael and Fianna Fáil. Homelessness raged throughout our city, people lay dying on hospital beds, and young people couldn't buy homes, but for some reason, the votes were still pouring in. Topping the poll wasn't about my ego, it was about sending out a message to the government and telling them that the people wanted change. My plan, if elected, was simple: stay true to myself, remain transparent, and don't allow politics to rot me to the core. I wasn't stupid either, I grew up with a target on my back, and now that target would be even bigger as people queued up to take me down, but I was ready for the fight, and ready to stand up for my people.

Throughout the count, I was surrounded by those who mattered to me. Tiernan, little six-month-old Sé, they were there for almost every minute of it, and Chelsea too. She was great with Séamus throughout and I didn't want him to miss this proud moment. Petesy Carroll, one of Ireland's original MMA journalists, was there, and Ariel Helwani, arguably the most famous MMA journalist in the world, kept ringing to check in on how the vote was going.

'I'm so happy for you, Paddy,' Ariel told me. 'Do you realise how big this is? This is huge, Paddy. Your people are voting for you. It's not just huge for you personally, but for the sport of MMA globally.'

Just the thought of being able to voice my opinion and make a difference at the local council, that filled me with a sense of pride and excitement. I joked that I would need a baseball cap with a rear-view mirror on it because of the number of people in politics who smile to your face and stab you in the back. It's the dirtiest game of all, but I was no fool. I was ready for the battle.

The official first count came through and I topped the poll. More people in Tallaght South had given me their first preference vote than anyone else. It was an amazing feeling to see the culmination of a lifetime of work for my area all coming together in the form of a name on a ballot paper with a number one written next to it. I was close but I wasn't in just yet. The first count and the calculation of transfers took much longer than expected, so after twelve hours at the count centre in Citywest, it became clear that it would be Sunday before I was elected. As I went home that night, emotionally and physically wrecked, I was proud of what I had achieved. Regardless of the outcome, the people had spoken and placed their faith in a council estate kid from Jobstown. I slept well that night and headed off back into Citywest the following morning for what I hoped would be my crowning moment.

The second and third count came through and I was still short a few votes, but edging closer to becoming elected. On the fourth count, I needed just four votes to be deemed elected by my people and each minute that passed seemed like an hour. Eight more hours of 'It's nearly time, it's nearly time' passed, and just as I was ready to collapse from exhaustion, word came through that I had made the quota on the sixth count. I was overcome with relief and hugged everyone as they congratulated me on my victory. It was finally time to be announced as an elected representative of Tallaght South.

As we walked over to the stage, I could feel the entire room's eyes looking at me. Some with disgust, others with respect, but I took it all in my stride with a big smile and a nod of the head. No one could deny this poll-topper his achievement. I could feel sweat crawling down my back, the hairs on my neck standing up and the cameras circling me. I could feel it again, something big happening.

'As the votes of Patrick Pearse Holohan exceed the quota, I deem him to be elected.'

As the words were read aloud in front of the crowd and cameras that had gathered in the count centre, I was overcome with emotion. I felt like crying and falling to my knees but I did my best to keep everything contained. My fellow party members and friends lifted me into the air as a round of applause filled the hall. I felt like I was back in front of the bright lights one more time, and I loved it.

'From council estate to councillor!' I screamed at the top of my lungs. This was my moment to thank the people of Tallaght, but also to show the world that anything is possible and that the Hooligan was here to stay. Be it in the octagon or in politics, I was always going to keep fighting until the end.

Councillor Paddy Holohan, 1-0 — May 2019

AFTERWORD

As I reflect on my life so far, I am filled with a sense of achievement and purpose. I now have a significant responsibility for my people and it's something that I will give my absolute all to make sure I deliver on. The main thing is that I am going to use the same rules I used in the UFC: to place importance on everything I do, stay true to myself and not get changed by the environment I'm running through or those around me. It didn't happen to me in MMA and it most certainly will not happen to me in politics.

One of the hardest things is that I'm a retired man starting a new career and I'm still only 31. I'm going to be sharing meetings and boardrooms with people who aren't from my class of people and I can already feel them looking down on me and judging me, waiting for me to fall. The competitive part of me loves it. It's another challenge. The doubt gives me energy and I want to absorb it all. These people are just angry and mad at themselves, and their insecurities shine through in how they look at and treat others. People always tell me to shut up but it's important I keep beating the drum and proving people wrong.

Two years ago, when my life was falling apart and I was at rock bottom, I knew I wasn't finished. I had more to give and that self-belief lit a fire in me. Politics helped me to rekindle that flame and light a fire under this election campaign. I needed to do this. I needed something incredible to keep me going. The gym was one fire and continues to blaze every day. We've gone from mats in a leisure centre hall to a 10,000 square foot gym with over 400 members. My own little palace. Some of our fighters are earning medals in European championships, others are fighting professionally, but most have been able to find a purpose in life, and for me, that's more valuable than any record or trophy.

It's the end of the beginning and now I'm ready to keep driving forward, rolling with the punches and proving everyone wrong. This is just a start, and I've found myself pointed in the right direction. Instead of sitting at home and wallowing in the despair of both my life and environment, I did something about it and now I'm an elected representative. No one can ever take that away, and that's important to me.

It's important for me to achieve things that can never be taken away from me. I earned the first Leaving Certificate in my family. I was the first Irish man to win a UFC fight on Irish soil. I was definitely the first haemophiliac on the entire planet crazy enough to fight professionally in the octagon. Now here I am, elected to public office after coming first in the polls.

I'm ready for whatever the world throws at me, and I feel like I'm just getting started.

ACKNOWLEDGEMENTS

Writing this book helped me more than I ever could have known it would have. It's not easy to face your life's actions straight on – it takes commitment and lots of effort, searching back and putting the pieces of the puzzle together. A huge part of why I did this was to try to instil hope in people and give a clear account of not only my career, life and upbringing, but also to give a view from someone who had the pleasure to be part of Irish fighting history. This is a story to be told to my clan for many years to come and one which will have the fortune to grow and get bigger like the modern-day MMA folklore it has become.

Thanks to Richie Barrett for taking this on and being so supportive throughout. We had our moments, but I can't thank you enough, and to Paul Fogarty for introducing us. Conor and his team at Gill, your patience and guidance has been amazing.

To the people I have shared mats, cages and rings with: I thank you and will be forever grateful for leaving parts of yourself alongside me in there. The many lessons I gained from coaches, and that team of people who blazed the Irish MMA trail, set the bar and paved the path for the future generations, that time made me the martial artist I am today.

The credit belongs to a few people who helped shape the man I am today. My mother, the strongest woman I know, I love you dearly and I want you to know its OK, I understand now, and I've got you for life. My uncle Paul, my grandfather and my aunt Margaret have been the most streetwise of teachers I could have ever hoped for. Willy, my grandad, filled my young mind with stories of ancient Ireland, politics, Mandela – the list is endless, and he instilled my integrity and hunger to learn. Mags gave me some of the happiest times of my childhood. She truly set my goal in motion – to have a real family and home was number one on the list when I found success. Waking to the smell of a fry and the Wolfe Tones filling the air of the house in Lenadoon and many other homes of hers always made me feel like they were my home too. My uncle Paul, or Jock as we called him, never saw me go without anything. He taught me very valuable lessons and showed me that the world isn't always what you think, and it can be nasty. He fine-tuned my gut instinct and he made me feel safe. He was my first coach, he taught me enough basics to fight back and I did. Without these people. I would not have made it to today.

I was blessed with a solid circle of friends: Macker, Dean, Adam, Finton and Robin kept me real and always gave me the straight answer I needed at times. Father Martin Hughes, I feel your good energies and thoughts you send to me, though I will never stop being amused by your worrying ways. Thanks for always looking out for me from that first day I walked into your office. The many closely attached to the journey: Shay and Jim Donnelly, Ollie, Lanny who followed me across the world and religiously came to watch me fight. You were there from the start to the end. We made life-long memories together and I hope yous hold them as close as I do.

To the Irish fans, and fans around the world: You filled me with energy and pride to carry that Irish flag. I have made it my honour to keep my work bond and in that UFC Octagon you guys were the extra arm for me. You will never beat the Irish.

My fiancée Chelsea and my two sons Tiernan and Séamus are my greatest achievements next to none. We only get one chance at this life and I'm truly grateful. I know the value of happiness, where and what it is in, and how to maintain it. Your support means the world to me.

When it's all said and done, the guy I have to thank the most is that inner voice: 'The Hooligan'. Understand that voice inside but don't let him control you with fear. Know yourself, and when the cage door closes, yous will be the men in the arena, nobody else.